HELL BENT

HELL BENT

How the Fear of Hell
Holds Christians Back from
a Spirituality of Love

BRIAN RECKER

Tarcher
an imprint of Penguin Random House
New York

Tarcher
an imprint of Penguin Random House LLC
1745 Broadway, New York, NY 10019
penguinrandomhouse.com

Tarcher is a registered trademark of Penguin Random House LLC, and Tarcher
with leaf design is a trademark of Penguin Random House LLC

Most Tarcher books are available at a discount when purchased in quantity
for sales promotions or corporate use. Special editions, which include
personalized covers, excerpts, and corporate imprints, can be created when
purchased in large quantities. For more information, please email
specialmarkets@penguinrandomhouse.com. Your local bookstore can also
assist with discounted bulk purchases using the Penguin Random House
corporate Business-to-Business program. For assistance in locating a
participating retailer, email B2B@penguinrandomhouse.com.

All Scripture quotations, unless otherwise indicated, are taken
from the Holy Bible, New International Version®, NIV®.
Copyright © 1973, 1978, 1984, 2011 by Biblica, Inc.®
Used by permission of Zondervan.
All rights reserved worldwide. www.zondervan.com
The "NIV" and "New International Version" are trademarks
registered in the United States Patent and
Trademark Office by Biblica, Inc.™

Scripture quotations marked ESV are taken from The ESV® Bible (The Holy
Bible, English Standard Version®), © 2001 by Crossway, a publishing ministry
of Good News Publishers. Used by permission. All rights reserved.

Scripture quotations marked KJV are taken from the
King James Version of the Bible.

Scripture quotations marked NRSV are taken from the New Revised Standard
Version Bible, copyright © 1989 the Division of Christian Education of the
National Council of the Churches of Christ in the United States of America.
Used by permission. All rights reserved.

Book design by Shannon Nicole Plunkett

Library of Congress Cataloging-in-Publication Data has been applied for.

Hardcover ISBN: 9780593853191
Ebook ISBN: 9780593853214

Printed in the United States of America
1st Printing

The authorized representative in the EU for product safety and compliance is
Penguin Random House Ireland, Morrison Chambers, 32 Nassau Street, Dublin
D02 YH68, Ireland, https://eu-contact.penguin.ie.

For my children,
for my own inner child,
and for the children still squirming
anxiously in the pews

Salvation is not precipitated by the terror of being consumed in hell: this terror itself places one in hell. . . . Salvation is not flight from the wrath of God; it is accepting and reciprocating the love of God. Salvation is not separation. It is the beginning of union with all that is or has been or will ever be.

—James Baldwin

Religion is for people who fear hell. Spirituality is for people who have been there.

—David Bowie

CONTENTS

INTRODUCTION

I t was a bright Sunday morning, and I smiled on my way to church. I'm an inconsistent churchgoer, but always a cheerful one. My history with church is complicated. After over eight years as an evangelical pastor, I don't consider myself an evangelical anymore. But I am still a Christian, and I do still go to church, at least when I feel like it. That's the key to smiling on the way to church—actually wanting to go. I don't do spiritual activities out of guilt anymore. I have absolutely no reason to do that, because I don't believe in a God who is out to punish me.

I still like going to worship gatherings because it helps me feel connected to myself and to other people, and it reminds me that we are all connected together through the Spirit of God. This Sunday, I was also going because I had invited another couple. Yes, I still invite people to church. Old habits die hard. But I didn't invite this couple out of guilt—I honestly don't care if anyone goes to church or not. Some people would be better served by a quiet morning alone with their dog, or a walk near a lake, or an intimate coffee date with a friend. Opportunities for spiritual connection abundantly surround us. No, I invited this couple because they're among the many people who have left evangelicalism behind but miss aspects of their former church communities. Such people often struggle to find a church that doesn't spark shame or religious guilt. I'm thankful that I've found a church community that welcomes and celebrates every kind of person, just as God made them to be, and I enjoy inviting others into it if it suits them too.

When I got to church, I was happy to meet my friends and excited to see what they'd think of the community. As the service ended, and we took Communion together, I wondered how the ritual was hitting my church-weary friends. Even when a church approaches this ancient Christian practice with a spirit of love and welcome, some people may still find that it transports them back to the terror they felt in their bodies when they were young, worried about whether they were "worthy enough" to partake of the body and blood of Christ.

I approached my friends cautiously after the service, curious if they found it refreshing, if they felt triggered by the experience, or anything in between. They told me that it was pretty good, for a church. But then the wife said, "Can I ask you a question?"

"Of course," I replied.

"If you don't believe in hell," she said with sincere curiosity, "then why do you still even go to church?"

On some level, her question surprised me. After all, what does going to church have to do with believing in hell? But of course I knew that for evangelical Christians, the answer is: just about everything.

Christianity has a hell problem. There is so much beauty and truth in Christianity. The golden rule is a brilliant piece of moral wisdom. The Beatitudes are a revolutionary way of looking at the world. Jesus's nonviolent path of enemy love inspired beacons of justice like Martin Luther King Jr. and the civil rights movement. And yet, no matter how much good you can find in it, at the end of the day, there is a big black hole right at the center: the belief that everyone who doesn't follow the right faith is going to hell to suffer for eternity.

This isn't a problem simply because I personally find it to be distasteful (though I do, and that's putting it mildly). This is a problem because hell—with the fear it inspires, the exclusivity it demands, the judgment it promotes, and the punitive God it portrays—corrupts Christian spirituality.

Evangelicals have sought to minimize the centrality of hell in recent years. Fire-and-brimstone preaching is less common than it used to be. The word *hell* is rarely heard in megachurches, which prefer "seeker-sensitive" messages. And yet, as long as hell is a part of the story, it will take center stage, even when we don't realize it. When my friend asked me why I still go to church even though I don't believe in hell, I realized her view of Christianity was, quite understandably, inseparable from fear and punishment. If there is no punishment to avoid, *what's the point?*

I gave her an honest answer: "I go to church because I'm one of those weird guys who *likes* going to church. I like singing the songs with everyone and wrestling with big spiritual ideas alongside my neighbors. But if you don't really like going to church, and you're going just in case you might go to hell, I really wouldn't worry about coming! Like seriously, it's fine." I smiled at her to make sure she knew I was not judging her (very normal) response to church. "Maybe go to brunch?" I suggested with a laugh. "Parkside has a decent Bloody Mary for seven dollars!"

She was a bit surprised, but as we talked, I was able to help her unravel some of the spiritual assumptions that were driving her behavior. She had left the church because she could no longer hold to exclusionary evangelical beliefs, but her spirituality was still governed by fear-based thinking and punishment avoidance. She felt in her gut that she should probably go back to church . . . *or else.*

There's a reason most Christians believe in hell, even though so few Bible verses describe anything like hell (something so eternally significant deserves more real estate, surely?) and even though almost nobody feels good about believing it. The whole system demands it. For most Christians, the whole point of Christian spirituality is *salvation.* Salvation from what? Salvation from hell. If you remove hell, there is no punishment to be saved from. For many people, that defeats the entire purpose of religion and spirituality. If you discard hell, the whole Christian story must be reconsidered.

Many of us already have been reconsidering the Christian faith. Between the rampant hypocrisy, the sex abuse cover-ups, and the evangelical embrace of Donald Trump, there are myriad reasons that people are streaming out of the church (evangelical or otherwise) and beginning a process of deconstruction. *Deconstruction* is the term used by a growing movement of people who have begun to investigate the premises of their faith with new eyes. Through that process, many people find they can no longer believe in a story that is centered on avoiding the eternal hell of a punishing God.

Rethinking hell was one of the first steps of my own deconstruction. I thought it was just one thread, but as I continued to pull it, the whole Christian faith seemed to be unraveling. I want to help you pull that thread, because I deeply hope that Christians—and everyone else—reject the doctrine of hell. But if the system is built on fear and punishment, ditching hell won't be enough. After all, if there is no hell, why was Jesus born? Why did Jesus die? Does sin matter if there's no hell? Is sin even a real thing? If there's no hell, is there a heaven? If there's no hell, what's the point of being a Christian? *If there's no hell, why the hell does any of it matter?*

This may surprise you, but I don't care if you're a Christian or not. If you're a Christian who is confused by the internal contradiction between hell and love, then this book is for you. If you've decided you're no longer a Christian but some aspects of the way of Jesus still stir you, then this book is for you too. And if you've left Christianity behind altogether but the fear of hell still creeps around on the edges of your spirituality, I'm writing for you as well. If you were raised in any number of church traditions, you may still be haunted by the specter of a punishing God. That makes sense, because it's the only God you've ever known. I hope this book helps you take a fresh look at the Christian story and recognize how a fear-based message may have affected your spiritual life. Maybe that will help you move forward in peace as an agnostic, an atheist, a Buddhist, or—who knows? There may be a healthy Christian spirituality for you yet. I'm not here to determine your path for you. I'm just here to tell you that hell doesn't have to be a part of it.

In this book, I'll explain why hell is not a biblical doctrine, but I want to go further than that. I want to trace how hell corrupts our spirituality to the very core. When I refer to the spirituality of hell, I mean more than just the belief that everyone who is not a born-again Christian will burn in hell. This is a toxic theology. But this toxic theology also creates a toxic *spirituality*—a misshapen way of relating to God, others, and yourself. The spirituality of hell is fear-based. It is motivated by avoiding punishment and rescuing other people from a punishing God. It results in guilt, shame, judgment, alienation, condemnation, othering, superiority, and paternalism—and it calls these things righteousness. If your spirituality is animated by hell, you may feel at your most holy right at the very moment you're behaving at your most unloving. I have had countless conversations with people whose parents disowned them in the name of saving their eternal souls. These parents literally cast their children aside and called it love. Their love is twisted by hell—it is hell bent.

For many of us, spirituality has been so defined by fear that if we uprooted punishment from our faith, there would be no positive spirituality left. We don't have a map for imagining spirituality outside of punishment. My goal in this book is to help you rewire your brain and start to imagine a spirituality of love beyond a punitive God. Thankfully Christianity is a rich tradition, with so much depth and beauty beyond hell, and Jesus is a spiritual teacher whose way of love is still worth imitating.

Let me orient you to what follows. In part I we will discuss the spirituality of hell: how hell corrupts Christian spirituality by disconnecting us from God, ourselves, and others. I will tell my own personal story, and you may see reflections of your own journey in mine.

In part II, we will deconstruct and reconstruct what the Bible says about hell, heaven, and the possibility of universal reconciliation. There is more to the story than what many of us were taught!

In the final section, we will reconsider the Christian story without punishment at the center and begin to dream about a spirituality of love. We will ask questions like, What's the point of Jesus if there's no hell? Why did Jesus die if not to save us from hell? What does it even mean to be saved? And how should Christians think about other religions if there is no hell?

So yes, this is a book about hell, but it's not just about hell. In fact, it is about the beautiful possibilities that can still exist for us within Christian spirituality. I believe Christian spirituality can reflect the very love that Jesus showed—a love that connects us to the best parts of ourselves. A love that can save the world. However, for many of us, including myself, hell is in the bedrock of the faith we inherited. Many of us feel that it is impossible to rip the fear out of the foundation without tearing down the entire house.

If we ditch hell, is there a Christianity left for us to salvage? Let's find out.

A FEW QUICK NOTES

My friend Scott Erickson likes to say that life is a combination of sacred moments and dick jokes. In "churchy" spaces, we tend to keep the sacred and profane as far away from each other as possible. This, in my opinion, is a failed experiment, the result of which is shame and hypocrisy. My personal opinion is that if spirituality is about being connected to my authentic self, that includes the part of me that says "fuck." So I'm talking about holy things in this book, and I will talk about them in the language that comes naturally to me, without censoring myself. Hopefully that will help you feel free to do the same—or at least know you're in a space where no one is judging you for your "unholy" thoughts.

Second note: I'm going to use varied pronouns for God. God is a universal Spirit and does not have genitals. Even though we know that God is genderless, many of us can't help but think of God as a big *guy*. A big *punishing* guy. It has been important for me to break this image by reminding myself that God is not only Father but also Mother. The Hebrew noun for God's Spirit is feminine. To that end, I will use they/

them as well as she/her pronouns for God in addition to he/him pronouns. You may find that my use of these pronouns makes you feel uncomfortable. Good! This is how we change our minds.

All right, babes, let's talk about hell.

Part I

A Spirituality of Hell

1.

THE MOST SOBERING REALITY

*How Hell Takes Center Stage
in Christianity*

If you are frightened into God, it is never the true God that you meet. If you are loved into God, you meet a God worthy of both Jesus and Christ. How you get there is where you arrive.

—Richard Rohr

The most sobering reality in the world today is that people are dying and going to hell today." These words echoed through the cavernous auditorium in the Bob Jones University chapel as five thousand students recited them together in a great rumble.

Bob Jones III, aka Dr. Bob, aka Triple Sticks, was the president of Bob Jones University, the (in)famous fundamentalist Christian college in Greenville, South Carolina, where I was a student. It was a custom of Dr. Bob's chapel messages to have us all stand up and speak that phrase in unison. I personally felt the motto was both heavy-handed and awkwardly phrased. I'd get stuck on how the word *today* was unnecessarily repeated. If this was his trademark phrase, shouldn't it be more tightly worded?

But even with the knowing cynicism of a nineteen-year-old pastor's kid who had heard this sort of thing his entire life, it was hard to dodge the impact of those words, which awakened the remembrance of a belief I preferred to keep buried. As a conservative Christian, of course I believed in hell. What else would I believe? This was a foundational belief for us all, and Dr. Bob knew that. His mantra was meant to remind us of what was at stake: everything. And even if I didn't like that, I didn't get to pick and choose which parts of Christianity I believed in. I thought that heaven came with hell—it was a package deal.

THE GOSPEL OF HELL

It is not so easy to define the Christian concept of hell. Christian beliefs about the afterlife have changed many times over the faith's two-thousand-year history, and they still vary significantly by denomination. Some denominations, like Catholicism, teach the existence of other post-death realms like purgatory, while others, like the Jehovah's Witnesses, believe that "unbelievers" will be annihilated out of existence.

What all of the views have in common is that hell is a place of punishment. Whether you believe it is a literal place of eternal torture (complete with real-ass flames) or a more figurative state of spiritual separation from God, hell is punitive. In fact, it is the worst possible punishment, for the longest possible amount of time. When I talk about hell in this book, I do not have one specific view in mind; rather, I am referring to the general Christian belief that God is going to punish everyone who is not a true Christian (however any particular denomination would define that).

I am the son of a fundamentalist Baptist pastor, which means I was raised with the conservative Protestant version of hell common in evangelicalism. Growing up, I believed that every person was going to stand before God when they died. God (who I imagined as a thousand-foot-tall, faceless, glowing man in a chair, due to the influence of the popular illustrated Chick tracts) would open up the book of life, and if someone's name wasn't in it, God would say, "Depart from me, I never knew you," and send that sorry son of a bitch to hell.

No matter how good you were, how many babies you kissed, or how many little old ladies you helped cross the street, you couldn't avoid hell on your own merits. No good works could do it, because your good works were tainted by what we called your *sin nature*. As a human, you were born inherently sinful, even before you had actually done anything wrong. By default, you were going to hell.

The only way out of hell was to become a Christian—to be born again. But for us that didn't just mean generally believing in Christianity, going to church, and saying your prayers. Rather, it meant believing in the very particular evangelical interpretation of Jesus. The most important part was having faith that Jesus died in your place and was punished for your sin. Either you believed that Jesus was punished for your sin on the cross, or you would be punished for your own sin in hell—*somebody* had to be punished. Evangelicals generally believe that not just some but most people will spend their eternity in hell—everyone without a "saving faith" in Jesus Christ. It was very important to be sure that you believed properly and sincerely, because the evangelical conception of hell is the worst fate imaginable. You're thrown into the lake of fire, where you're burned forever but never consumed; your eternal soul goes on existing, just to experience the infinite pain of your rejection of salvation.

This is the good news of the gospel of Jesus Christ. *Thanks be to God.*

Now, many modern evangelicals try to tone this picture down in various ways. For example, Tim Keller, who was considered one of the most intellectual and least fearmongering figures in evangelicalism until his recent passing, believed that the flames of hell are metaphorical, not literal. However, he made it clear that he was not going soft on hell: "To say that the Scriptural image of hellfire is not wholly literal is *of no comfort whatsoever*. The reality *will be far worse than the image*. . . . Away from the favor and face of God, we literally, horrifically, and endlessly fall apart" (emphasis mine).

Whether the details are literal or metaphorical, the punishment is horrific. It has to be. The punishment is the point.

PLAYING THE HELL CARD

"The most sobering reality in the world today is that people are dying and going to hell today." Dr. Bob would usually have us recite this mantra during the last chapel service before we went home for Thanksgiving, Christmas, or summer breaks. He was preparing us to head back home, where we would likely run into "unbelievers" among our friends and family. He was training us to see those moments through the lens of eternity, with the recognition that every person at that holiday get-together had an eternal soul; they were going to live somewhere forever. Whether that somewhere was a place of eternal torment or eternal bliss was something that we were supposed to become very invested in. It absolutely *was* our business what other people believed, because how could we say we loved someone and yet be indifferent on the issue of them burning for eternity? So, standing in a long tradition of fundamentalist preachers, Dr. Bob played the hell card, knowing exactly what feelings he would produce in us. A deep inner fear, with a thick layer of guilt.

"When was the last time you gave someone the gospel?" Dr. Bob would ask. "Or led someone to the Lord? Don't you care about your family and friends who don't believe? You say that you do, but you seem to stay conveniently comfortable when you spend time with them, almost as if you've forgotten the most important truth of all—that if they died today, they would spend an eternity in the white-hot flames of hell, and the truth is you didn't do a single thing to stop it!"

The sense of guilt I would feel during sermons like this was such a familiar sensation in church that, from a young age, I associated that feeling with true spirituality. In other words, I felt at my most spiritual when I was taking hell the most seriously. In my heart, I would recommit to placing this sobering reality at the center of my actions, determined to strengthen my own faith and save other people's souls.

This was not an easy thing to do. The belief that most of the people in the world are going to endure obscene suffering for eternity is a difficult thing to keep front of mind! Unless you wanted to be *very* weird socially, you had to compartmentalize it. If you believed in hell, you learned to accept cognitive dissonance. Angry preachers screaming fire-and-brimstone sermons on street corners to urban passersby may have sounded crazy, but they were living perfectly in line with their beliefs; I, believing in hell but not spending every waking moment trying to save people from it, was not. Their socially abrasive street evangelism was perfectly sensible in light of a truth that I preferred to keep tucked in the back of my mind.

If hell was real, we should have all been screaming about it.

If you've never spent time as an evangelical Christian, you may be tempted to think that they revel in the reality of hell or take joy in the fact that everyone except them is completely screwed. This is not the case. Most evangelicals don't like thinking about it at all, because they're not sociopaths. Unfortunately, even though we avoided dwelling on it, that actually made us *feel like worse Christians*. After all, if hell was real, we needed to be talking about it *more*, not less. If the stakes are really that high, and if we really believed that everyone who didn't believe in Jesus was going to experience the ultimate level of suffering for an infinite amount of time, then it was *hateful*, not loving, to avoid talking about hell.

The celebrity magician and outspoken atheist Penn Jillette had a viral video in which he pointed out the hypocrisy of Christians who said they believed in hell but weren't constantly talking about it. "I don't respect that at all," he said. "If you believe that there's a heaven and hell and people could be going to hell . . . and you think that it's not really worth telling them this because it would make it socially awkward . . . how much do you have to hate somebody to not proselytize?"

Jillette was right, of course, that if an evangelical was living in integrity—bringing their behavior in line with their beliefs—they'd be shouting the gospel of hell from the rooftops. His challenge exposes the cognitive dissonance that many evangelicals experience when it comes to the doctrine of hell. But this cognitive dissonance isn't the true problem; rather, it points to a deeper problem with the doctrine itself. I believe that most evangelicals would prefer to avoid preaching to others about hell not because it's awkward or because their faith is weak but because they intuitively know it is a wicked doctrine that does not reflect the love of God.

Their intuition is right.

A SPIRITUALITY OF HELL

Hell, being the worst possible thing that could ever happen to anybody, has a way of crowding out other spiritual priorities. It sucks the air out of the room when it comes to any positive vision for spirituality. It shapes Christian spirituality in its punishing image.

For example, evangelicals often speak of good deeds like caring for the poor as a distraction from the "main thing." After all, no earthly justice is as important as keeping people out of hell. What good is feeding the hungry if we don't save their souls? Alleviating worldly suffering means nothing if we don't save people from the eternal suffering that is waiting for them.

This focus on hell doesn't just make conservative evangelicals ignore social welfare—it frequently causes them to actively oppose it. When I was a pastor, I once had an argument with another pastor who believed that the government shouldn't provide welfare programs because that took the opportunity away from the church. "If the church was providing for the poor instead of the government," he said, "then it would open up an opportunity to give them the gospel, which is what they really need. The government might lift people out of poverty, but it won't save them from hell!" His view was not unique; in fact, it is incredibly common in evangelicalism. One of the hallmarks of toxic theology is that it causes you to reason yourself out of doing obviously good things for people in the name of your theology.

I argued with him, saying, "We should be serving and loving people for love's own sake! If we're only doing works of love to save people from hell, then our love isn't pure—it has an agenda!" I don't know why I was surprised by his line of thinking, though. Of course our loving deeds had an agenda. How could they not? If you believe hell is real, then hell will always set the agenda.

Because it was such a severe and all-encompassing reality, hell had a way of shaping all our spiritual priorities. Being a good neighbor didn't have to mean caring for the vulnerable in our communities or learning to embrace and center marginalized people; it could just mean that you tried to keep your neighbor out of hell. This made hell a trump card. The most unloving beliefs could be called loving when they were done in the name of saving people from hell. Even the very definition of what it meant to love was poisoned by hell.

Here is a true and common story to show you what I mean. My friend June came out as a lesbian in her forties, after deconstructing her evangelical Christianity. She was the daughter of an evangelical pastor, and her family had already had a difficult time with the fact that she'd left the church. When she told them that she was gay and planned on bringing her partner to Thanksgiving that year, the pot of fear boiled over. They drew the line there. She was not welcome to come with her partner. June sobbed to me on the phone about this, asking me how they could uninvite their own daughter from Thanksgiving. "How could they say they loved me on the same phone call where they rejected me?" she asked me. I told her that I wasn't sure if it helped to hear, but they almost certainly did love her—it's just that, unfortunately, a spirituality of hell twists and corrupts love into something that feels a lot more like hate.

This story is familiar to many queer children of evangelical parents. In the name of saving their children from hell, these parents have excluded, condemned, disowned, and otherwise traumatized their own kids. And I'm sure that just about every time this has happened, those parents assured their children (and themselves) that they were doing these things out of love. June's parents probably felt that they were doing the hard thing that needed to be done. In their mind, her sexual orientation was "unrepentant sin," which meant she was going to hell. They felt they were being good Christians by prioritizing their daughter's soul over her momentary happiness. They likely felt at their *most spiritual*, even as they wounded their daughter's spirit. This is the spirituality we're living out when hell is in the foundation.

Based on the way many Christians speak about hell and punishment, it would be easy to think that hell was Jesus's central message. I will explain in depth in later chapters how that couldn't be further from the truth, but I think it's also helpful to look at the *point Jesus was making* when he did speak about something like hell. It is almost always the exact opposite of the point that evangelicals are making, and reveals almost the exact opposite priorities.

For example, one of the most commonly cited sayings of Jesus on hell is Matthew 25:46, where the wicked "go away to eternal punishment, but the righteous to eternal life." But if we zoom out and look at what Jesus was talking about in these verses, we see that it has nothing to do with "becoming a Christian," believing the right doctrines, or Jesus being punished in our place so we could be forgiven. This passage is about our behavior in this world, and specifically our behavior toward "the least of these" (Matthew 25:45). Jesus is warning us that when we neglect vulnerable, marginalized people, we create hell for ourselves and for other people.

You don't need to die to see that this is true. You only have to open your eyes to a world on fire with climate change, where the gap between rich and poor continues to increase, and the wealthiest country in the history of the world spends its riches on bombs instead of health care. Going by Jesus's priorities, the most sobering reality in the world today isn't a hell that waits for us when we die. It is the poor being neglected, the hungry going without food, the immigrants being refused at the border, and the incarcerated being ignored. It is a hell of our own making, right here and now. Jesus was not "hell bent" on saving souls for the afterlife but on bringing the wholeness and love of God into *this* world, on *this* side of eternity.

But the evangelical doctrine of hell makes it very difficult to have the priorities of Jesus. Hell has the gravitational pull of a black hole, sucking in and crushing every other priority under its weight. It leaves us with a spirituality of fear instead of love, one that is focused on the afterlife at the expense of this life.

As I have begun to unpack the impacts this doctrine has

had on my spiritual development, I see that fear and disconnection were cemented into the foundation of my faith from
the very beginning, damaging my relationships with God,
with other people, and even with myself. And I see that the
same is true for many other people coming from a variety of
different Christian backgrounds, who are on a variety of different deconstruction journeys.

For those of us who were raised with this kind of spirituality, evangelical or otherwise, there is work to do. If we want
to reclaim a healthy, connected relationship with God, ourselves, and other people, we will first have to deconstruct the
fear-based spirituality that has so damaged us.

2.

LOVE GOD, OR ELSE

*How a Spirituality of
Hell Disconnects Us from God*

What we're saved from, in biblical terms of salvation, is God himself. God is the one who saves us through his Son, but he sends his Son to save us from Him.

—Popular evangelical teacher R. C. Sproul

Jesus says in Mark 12 that the greatest commandment is to love God with all our heart, soul, mind, and strength, and that the second is to love our neighbor as ourselves. In these brief sentences, I find the core of a spirituality that continues to resonate with me: Spirituality is about loving God, others, and myself. I consider anything that deepens my connection with God, others, and myself to be a spiritual practice.

Conversely, the behaviors and beliefs that lead to disconnection from God, others, and the self are *barriers* to love and healthy spirituality. To use biblical language, you might even call these forces of disconnection *sin*. When I consider how the doctrine of hell has affected my spirituality, I can see many ways that it has caused this harmful, even sinful, disconnection. In later chapters, I will explain in detail why hell is not sound biblical or theological doctrine, but before I do that, I think it's important for us to spend some time thinking about how the fear of hell has spiritually alienated us, starting with how it has alienated us from God.

This is urgent for Christians because Jesus said that loving God is the most important thing a human being can do, and it is impossible to have a truly loving connection with God under the threat of punishment. And if you no longer identify as Christian, keep reading—this is still an essential step in reconnecting to whatever higher power you do believe in (if any).

WORKING ON YOUR RELATIONSHIP WITH GOD

Evangelicals talk a lot about their "relationship with God." Growing up, whenever I felt a sense that I should be doing internal work to grow spiritually, perhaps after a week of Christian camp or a particularly convicting sermon, I would say that I needed to "work on my relationship with God." This language is so pervasive that the classic youth group break-up line is actually "I just need to focus on my relationship with God right now." (Even the horniest high school boy at Young Life can't argue with that zinger.)

The idea is that you don't just sit in the pews and sing a few hymns on Sunday, then go back to thinking about bills and chores for the rest of the week. Instead, you have a close personal relationship with God, communicating with God every day, sharing your deepest secrets and joyful moments with God, making God an integral part of your life much the way you would with a family member or close friend. But in a spirituality of hell, there can be nothing healthy about the dynamic of your relationship with God; it is poisoned with fear from the very beginning.

The threat of hell doesn't have to be explicitly stated, and, depending on what kind of church you attend, it may not be. Most modern megachurches, for example, avoid discussing hell as much as possible. You can find it in the statements of faith on their websites, but you will rarely hear it mentioned in a Sunday sermon. They're trying to be "seeker sensitive," and they don't want to scare anyone away too quickly. Instead, churches like this emphasize the idea of "salvation"— but salvation from what? From hell. When newcomers and young children are encouraged to be born again, why are they told being born again is necessary? Because of hell. For evangelicals and for many other Christians, *every decision to be in a relationship with God begins with hell.*

In my experience growing up as a fundamental Baptist, hell was not lurking in the background—it was center stage. I made my first decision for Jesus after learning about the two options I had for an eternal destination, and I have to say, it didn't feel like much of a choice. This was especially true because I was so young; many adult Christians have trained themselves to avoid thinking about hell, but for children, the idea is often formative and horrifying.

The list of people who qualified for hell according to our standards was long. As fundamentalists, we thought even many Christians wouldn't be spared. Certainly not Catholics—my dad called Catholicism a cult and said the pope was possibly the antichrist. This meant my best friend, Alex, and his Catholic family were in trouble, along with anyone else who wasn't "born again" to our specifications. Before bed, or even sometimes at mealtime, we would pray for them and our other friends and relatives who were "unsaved."

Due to how narrow the gate seemed to be, I was constantly worried about my own qualifications. I was "saved" for the first time when I was five years old, but that was far from the last time. We had yearly revival meetings where an evangelist would come to town and whip us into a frenzy about our salvation. Despite (or perhaps because of) their scare tactics, these meetings were always entertaining, and they made you feel something.

My favorite evangelists had gimmicks. Stan Harris was a tenth-degree karate black belt who would chop through cinder blocks before preaching down the house, hollering and sweating through the gi he would wear for his demonstration. I loved his preaching, in a twisted way, because it also horrified me. I would feel dirty, sinful, and in need of being forgiven—I was transfixed.

"And with every head bowed and every eye closed,"

Harris (and really every evangelist throughout my childhood) would say, "with no looking around the room, it's just you and the Lord right now. If tonight, on the way home, a car accident were to take you into eternity, and you found yourself standing before the Lord, if he asked you why he should let you into his kingdom, would you have an answer?"

I could picture it: standing before a God of nightmares blazing with holiness, the gatekeeper of heaven, the one who had such stringent specifications for who was in and who was out.

"And with every head bowed and every eye still closed, if you're here tonight and you want to be ready, if you want to know for sure that you are safe and secure in the blood of Jesus, I want you to pray this prayer in your heart."

I always hated this part. The fear made it impossible not to pray the prayer with him. Just in case. Every single time. Every single year.

"OH, holy God," Harris would pray, while I echoed the words reverently in my heart, "we know that our sins have disqualified us from your gracious presence and that every single one of us deserves hell. But we plead the blood of your son, Jesus Christ. Please, God, cleanse us of our sin, that we might be born again to love and follow you. In Jesus's name, amen!"

After a pause, he continued: "Now, if you prayed that prayer with me tonight, I want you to raise your hand."

Those fuckers. The evangelists did that every time, and I always fell for it.

As the pastor's son, I found the hand-raising moment incredibly embarrassing. I was already supposed to have been born again. I didn't want anyone in the congregation to see me do it, over and over, thinking that I just got saved for the

347th time. But if I *didn't* raise my hand, wouldn't that make my decision for Christ disingenuous?

As you can imagine, this constant fear grew exhausting. Eventually, I learned how to avoid thinking about it directly and to live with a constant sense of insecurity that I pushed down into the back of my mind. But at any point, if I began to drift away from Christian devotion, the fear would quickly rush back in. The fear would remind me that I had better work on my relationship with God. Or else.

A TOXIC RELATIONSHIP WITH GOD

The consequence for not working on a normal relationship with another person is disconnection within that relationship. The thing that motivates us to work on a healthy, satisfying relationship, whether it be with our romantic partners, family members, or friends, is not that we are afraid they'll punish us (although that may be the case in an immature or unhealthy relationship)—it's that we want to be connected to them, not disconnected. Healthy, loving relationships are sustained by the desire we feel to be with the other person and the positive benefits we receive from the relationship—not by a fear of punishment.

The best relationships lead to growth. This is why we invest in our loving connections: They're good for us. When you love someone, you want to see them be the best version of themselves, and in a healthy mutual relationship, this desire is returned. Psychiatrist M. Scott Peck beautifully defines love as "the will to extend one's self for the purpose of nurturing one's own or another's spiritual growth." In other words, we seek connection in order to help each other bloom into the best versions of ourselves. This is the positive reason we pursue connection. If we pursue connection to God, it should be because this connection will cause us to grow in love; as 1 Thessalonians 3:12 says, "May the Lord make your love increase and overflow for each other and for everyone else."

Unfortunately, in a spirituality of hell, this positive reason to stay connected to God is overshadowed by the negative reason. If hell is real and God punishes people for failing to be in a proper relationship with God, then connection to God is not about growing in God's love; it is about avoiding God's punishment. And if you ask any therapist or relationship expert, What do you call a relationship where you're not allowed to leave or the other person will punish you? they will tell you: That's a toxic relationship.

When I left home and graduated from Bob Jones, I remained evangelical but moved away from fundamentalism. I was sick of the fire-and-brimstone preaching, the bad haircuts,* and the all-around bad vibes. I found churches that allowed Christian rock bands, let the preachers wear jeans, and didn't mention hell in every other sermon. I remember the relief in my spirit when I found evangelical churches that centered the grace and love of God instead of hell. Finally, I could focus on the true heart of Christianity: God's love. However, I soon realized that despite new talking points, almost all these churches had the same doctrine of hell that I was raised with, and the same long list of people going there (though there was more leeway extended to the Catholics at least). They changed the Sunday-morning emphasis from

---

* At Bob Jones, I got many demerits for "uncheckable" hairstyles. Hair had to be off of the ears and collar, and "prayer captains" and "hall leaders" were constantly on the prowl for shaggy cuts. My junior year, they also banned the popular "faux-hawk" style, which of course I was proudly rocking at the time. I remember being stopped by a hall leader who told me I was in trouble because I had a "fox-hawk," as he mispronounced it.

fear to love, and they dropped the scare tactics and manipulative altar calls, but they didn't change the underlying assumption that God sends "unbelievers" to hell. In what were ostensibly more liberal churches, the relationship with God was still toxic, even as they claimed that it was all based on love.

In fact, claiming that a relationship with a punishing God is actually all based on love is a kind of gaslighting. I know, I know, I'm going heavy on the therapy speak. But hear me out, I think it's warranted here. In the field of psychology, *gaslighting* is the term for a form of manipulation that an abuser uses to sow self-doubt in the victim's mind, causing the victim to doubt their own intuition and sense of reality. When forced to confront their own behavior in some way, a gaslighter might say something like, "You're lying, that never happened" or "There you go again, making up crazy stories to make me look bad." When an abusive husband tells his wife, "Don't be ridiculous, I love you! *You're* the one who's hurting *me*," that's gaslighting. Over time, the victim starts to question their own thoughts and memories, so that, in addition to the abuse itself, they have the added burden of feeling "crazy."

Much like that abusive husband, the evangelical church told us Christianity was all about love. I was taught God loved me and accepted me by pure grace, and in response, I was supposed to love God. I certainly wanted that to be true. I wanted a God who loved me, and I wanted to be the kind of person who loved God for God's own sake. But how could God truly love me and at the same time be willing to let me undergo torment for eternity? And how could I truly love God when doing otherwise would mean consigning my soul to hell? The foundation of our relationship with God is the fear of burning forever, yet religious leaders turn around and tell us, "Actually, this is love. In fact, it's the holiest and most perfect love possible! God loves you! And if you question that, you might not really love God. In fact, you might not even be a Christian . . . and you know what that means." That's textbook gaslighting. And like textbook gaslighting victims, many Christians suffer not only the fear of hell itself but also the additional burden of feeling sinful or heretical if they question whether this is all really about love.

NO PUNISHMENT IN LOVE

Our relationship with God isn't supposed to be toxic. I believe a loving, healthy relationship with God is not only possible—it is a foundation for a wholehearted life (I will explore what this can look like in the last chapter of this book)! But the constant threat of punishment has misshapen our perception of what God is like, giving us a false view of God that is incompatible with the God Jesus called *Abba*, or *Father*. As a result, we are disconnected from the true God, the God of love. As Franciscan priest and author Richard Rohr says, "If you are frightened into God, it is never the true God that you meet . . . how you get there is where you arrive." Many of us met God in fear, and we did not arrive in love.

In 1 John 4:18, John the evangelist writes, "There is no fear in love. But perfect love drives out fear, because fear has to do with punishment." In a spirituality of hell, our love from God and for God is tainted by fear. And the reason is simple: It "has to do with punishment." Punishment distorts the pure reality of God's all-encompassing love. John concludes the verse by saying, "The one who fears is not made perfect in love." Being "made perfect in love" means experiencing the kind of growth, nurturing, and well-being we find in healthy, loving relationships. John says that this kind of ove is not compatible with fear and punishment. Fear freezes us. It destroys connection and makes growth impossible. It shrinks and diminishes us.

If God is love, then God seeks our growth in love. If we are to grow in the love of God, we must be safe to make mistakes, to learn, to wander, to explore, and to be curious. We must be safe to question what we have been told by religious leaders who claim to speak for God. We must be safe to listen to the voice of our own conscience and trust that a God who is love will not damn us for questioning exclusionary theology or abusive churches. Our hearts bloom and open with love where we are safe. The threat of punishment makes God's love unsafe.

A punishing God can only be loved in the way a child can love an abusive parent. It is a love soaked through with fear. As feminist theorist bell hooks writes in her book *All About Love*, "There is nothing that creates more confusion about love in the minds and hearts of children than unkind and/or cruel punishment meted out by the grown-ups they have been taught they should love and respect. Such children learn early on to question the meaning of love, to yearn for love even as they doubt it exists." If God is both love and a punisher, we learn to question the meaning of love. We may not realize it, but we can even begin to doubt that love exists. If God is punishing, then reality is fundamentally punishing, not loving.

Children who are forced to love in this way learn distorted ways of showing and receiving love. Hooks writes of an encounter she had with an angry man who "bragged about the aggressive beatings he had received from his mother, sharing that 'they had been good for him.'" She "interrupted and suggested that he might not be the misogynist woman-hater he is today if he had not been brutally beaten by a woman as a child." If God's love includes punishment, then we start to believe our love can include punishment.

Conservative Christians have attempted to explain how God can send people to hell and still be loving. They will tell you that God loves us and doesn't want us to go to hell. If anyone goes to hell, it is because they rejected God's love. If we turn down God's free gift of salvation, it is because of *our own* sin and stubbornness; it isn't God's fault. And sure, if you cobble together enough doctrines that the church has come up with over the centuries, you can make this kind of theological defense. But there is no emotional defense. No amount of theological mental gymnastics can make fear and love coexist, or help us create a genuine connection with a punishing God.

For me, the simplest way to think about how absurd these theological arguments are is to imagine my relationship with my own children. I would never condemn my kids to a life of punishment and suffering, even if they rejected a relationship with me. My love for them is not conditional on them responding to me in the way that I want. Some evangelicals might respond that I should not compare my love as a father with God's love, because God's ways are "higher than [our] ways" (Isaiah 55:8–9). They are right. God's love is far more merciful than mine. Despite my best intentions, my love sometimes includes punishment, but there is no punishment in a God of perfect love.

Christians can know that this is true, because we learn what God's love is like by looking at Jesus, who commands us to love our enemies and do good for those who harm us (Luke 6:27). How nonsensical would it be if God didn't take God's own advice? We are told to love our enemies, not punish them, because punishment only pushes people further away, but love changes people; love turns enemies into friends. It is

God's love for us that softens our hearts, that draws us in and reconciles us to God. Punishment cannot do that; only love can do that. If God were a punisher, God could not do the work of reconciliation.

As many of us look back on our spiritual journeys, we see that the fear of hell was the hook that got us into Christianity in the first place, and even as we attempted to cultivate a relationship with God, we did it under the threat of punishment. Is it any surprise that many of us wonder if there was ever anything genuine in our connection to God? Christianity promised us a loving relationship with God, but hell has robbed us of it.

It has also, as we'll see in the next chapter, robbed us of our relationship with ourselves.

3.

BORN THIS WAY

*How a Spirituality of
Hell Disconnects Us from Ourselves*

We were innocent before we started feeling guilty; we were in the light before we entered into the darkness; we were at home before we started to search for a home. Deep in the recesses of our minds and hearts there lies hidden the treasure we seek.

—Henri Nouwen

just want to stop hating myself." From a Zoom square on my computer, Jake opened his heart and told me his story. Three months ago, he had come out as gay to his wife. They had three small children together—triplets! He felt horrible that he had lied about his sexuality not only to her but also to himself. Now they had a beautiful, growing family, and he felt torn between living authentically and continuing to shove down his feelings for the sake of the traditional family structure he wanted so badly.

Shame has a powerful way of keeping us from seeing ourselves clearly. Jake had only recently come to the point where he could even acknowledge to himself that he was gay. He knows now that he has always been gay, but growing up in evangelicalism, the shame was too great and the cost too high to admit it. As he and his wife evolved spiritually, they ultimately left their evangelical church. Only after they were free from that environment did Jake give himself permission to be honest about his own sexuality. It was frightening, but he knew the truth needed to come out, no matter how disruptive it would be to his family. After a period of hurt and mourning, his wife began to be supportive. She wanted him to be happy. She wanted them to learn how to co-parent together. Perhaps some part of her had always known. She had begun to accept it.

But Jake couldn't accept himself. He felt guilty about what he saw as robbing his children of the chance to grow up in a traditional household with happily married parents who stayed together. But more than that, he felt shame about *who he was.* "Even my wife doesn't hate me and wants me to be happy, but for some reason, I don't know how to feel that for myself," he told me on our call. "I want to celebrate who I am and feel hopeful about my future, but I can't help it. I feel dirty. I feel wrong. I feel broken."

I knew the feeling of brokenness he was talking about. Those of us who were raised in evangelicalism were taught that we were "born in sin." The doctrine of "original sin" means that we inherit sin from Adam; it is our birthright. You were a sinner, deserving of hell, before you even took your first breath. It is a part of who you are. This idea was wielded like a medieval claymore, and brutish preachers swung that heavy sword at us each week in their sermons, decimating any sense of confidence in ourselves.

These preachers had their handful of favorite verses. They loved to remind us that our hearts were "desperately wicked" (Jeremiah 17:9, KJV). That even our righteous deeds were like "filthy rags," detestable in God's sight (Isaiah 64:6). When these hyperbolic prophetic passages were written thousands of years ago, they were directed at wicked kings and violent empires, but our animated preachers plucked them out of context and used them very effectively against anyone with a pulse, including children. Those of us who grew up under this kind of dogma felt like perpetual pieces of shit simply for existing. No wonder we believed in hell; we were taught that was where we belonged and that it was only because of God's extraordinary love that some of us might make it to heaven, despite our inherent badness.

If we go by Jesus's definition, healthy spirituality consists of love for God, one's neighbor, and oneself. We've looked at how the doctrine of hell corrupts our relationship with God.

Now let's look at how it corrupts our relationship with ourselves.

(DON'T) FOLLOW YOUR HEART

It's no surprise to me that Jake had a difficult time loving and accepting himself. He had been told that his very essence as a human being was worthy of eternal suffering, and his sexual orientation was a constant reminder of the innate sinfulness that condemned him. Like Jake, I learned to believe the worst about myself. Despite Jesus's insistence that the second greatest commandment (which is actually held in an equal place with the greatest commandment) is to love your neighbor *as yourself,* self-love was never given much priority. In all my years in the church, I never heard a single sermon about how to love yourself. In fact, I was explicitly taught to do just the opposite.

I grew up being told that "following my heart" was one of the worst things I could do, because it would inevitably lead me astray. We were meant to hate our fleshly desires and doubt our thoughts and feelings. I remember my dad pointing out the "dangerous messages" in Disney movies like *Mulan* and *Tarzan*, which emphasized trusting your heart and listening to yourself. I was told that I should trust in God's word alone, because my heart was "deceitful above all things" (Jeremiah 17:9). My inner voice was something to drown out and ignore.

Instead of learning to have a healthy relationship with myself, I learned to search my heart for sin and to make myself hyperaware of my shortcomings. The guilt and self-doubt that I'd experience were seen as good things. They were evidence of God's work in my heart and the conviction of the Holy Spirit. In the spirituality of hell, we are at our most spiritual not when we are loving the holiest parts of our-selves or giving ourselves grace and room to grow, but when we are despising the most broken parts of ourselves.

This compulsive self-loathing was especially vivid during the practice of Communion. Before we received the sacred elements of Welch's grape juice and the dryest cracker you've ever had, the preacher (for me, this was typically my dad) would remind us in the gravest of terms, "God's word tells us that before we come to the table, we must examine ourselves, lest we take his body and blood in an *unworthy manner*." If the preacher was feeling extra spicy that week, he might even add, "God's word warns us that if you eat and drink unwor-thily, the consequences are severe. 'This is why some of you are weak and sick, and some people have died'!"

These words of warning come from 1 Corinthians 11, in which the apostle Paul scolds a church in Corinth for the way they're holding Communion. But his problem is not that sin-ful individuals are taking Communion. His problem is that instead of eating the Lord's Supper together, the rich mem-bers of the church were having "private suppers" that ex-cluded the poor members (1 Corinthians 11:21). Paul is condemning turning a communal rite into something judg-mental and exclusionary. But that's not how our church in-terpreted it. We interpreted it as a warning to search our wicked hearts for sin before we take Communion, lest we "drink judgment on [our]selves" (1 Corinthians 11:29).

During the long moments of prayerful silence that fol-lowed the preacher's exhortation, I would contemplate and enumerate my sins, trying not to think too much about the vague but menacing consequences if I ate that dusty cracker without a properly devoted heart. Sickness and death were on the table, of course, but it was hell that loomed in the back-ground over everything. During these times of monthly examination, I repented my guts out and racked up another few dozen salvation prayers.

It's hard to say which of my sins plagued me as a six- or seven-year-old—what could a child that young possibly have done wrong? Only a very twisted theology could claim little kids deserve eternal torment. It's such a hard idea to swallow that some evangelicals actually suggest there's an "age of accountability," just to take the edge off a bit. Essentially, this means that even though we are all born evil and worthy of hell, God might have mercy on unbelieving children who die, up to a certain age, at which point they become fully responsible for their sins and are cleared hot for damnation. Nobody knew what that age was, because this teaching is not found anywhere in scripture—it's entirely made up, to make the concept of hell slightly more palatable—so I remember hoping, at seven or eight years old, that I was still in my grace period, just in case something happened to me. Y'know, normal seven-year-old thoughts.

Even if I hadn't committed any horrible sins, I was aware of my sin nature as a sort of rebellious feeling in my gut. I was always able to find evidence of sin in my life if I searched for it, and boy, did I search for it. For example, whenever I learned about "curse words," I enjoyed repeating them to myself when I was alone, even though I knew I wasn't allowed. Now, having kids of my own, I know this is a natural developmental practice of boundary testing and play. It's how kids learn that some adult rules are arbitrary and don't actually cause real harm. I wasn't evil—I was growing up! But during those times of self-examination, I remember thinking that my recitation of euphemisms and low-level swear words was a testament to my sinful will and wicked heart. This is how a spirituality of hell destroys our relationship with ourselves from a young age.

SIN, SEXUALITY, AND SEARS CATALOGS

As I grew older, I had much more to feel guilty about—not because I started going around stealing things or hurting people but because I developed a normal human sexuality. Conservative Christianity tells us our very nature condemns us to hell, but it reserves a special wrath for anything related to sex.

Through puberty, those times of self-examination hit differently. I would squirm in my pew, remembering whatever preteen sex fantasy I had the night before, feeling dirty and damnable. I was taught that Christians were meant to be growing in holiness through a process of sanctification in which we became more and more like Jesus. If there was one thing I knew about the evangelical Jesus, it was that he did not have the lingerie section of the Sears catalog hidden under his mattress! By the time my hormones started raging, I had already "been saved" for five or six years, so this struggle with my sexuality made me feel like I was going in the wrong direction. Of course, we knew that all Christians would still occasionally sin, but I was told that a Christian would not "continue in sin." Touching myself every night was not very "new creation" of me. This naturally led me to question whether or not I could truly be a Christian—and you know what happens to people who aren't truly Christian.

Like many Christians, I felt my sexuality was evidence of what I always knew to be true: I was a wicked sinner, and I needed to be saved. I didn't know how to stop myself from experiencing my budding sexual desires, so I did what I knew I could. I prayed more salvation prayers with more fervor, hoping that this time it would "take," so I could be rid of the nagging guilt and fear for my soul. But it felt increasingly obvious that these sexual urges were not simply going to disappear. Praying a fresh "sinner's prayer" week after week grew exhausting. Something had to give. Eventually, I learned how to compartmentalize the cognitive dissonance. I allowed my-self to disassociate when it came to my sexuality. I would indulge and then pretend it hadn't happened and just move on with my life. On Sunday mornings, I did my best to pretend that none of that nighttime mess-around had ever happened. That was another guy. This is "Sunday morning Brian," and *he is spiritual.*

I believe this divided self is a normal part of the spiritual-ity of hell, when it comes to sexuality or any other aspect of human existence. What other option do we have? If the things that feel dirty about us—whether they are actual toxic behav-iors or just unremarkable aspects of our humanity—put us in danger of being destroyed by God, then *of course* we will learn to hide them. No wonder church people are commonly known as hypocrites; punishing environments breed hypoc-risy. Safety is required for authenticity.

This cosmic guilt trip from the church was rarely directed at actually harmful behavior like sexual assault. It was nor-mal, healthy human sexuality that was so despised. In retro-spect, telling children going through puberty that their natural biological development could cause them to be tortured for eternity is a pretty wild thing to do! Supposedly, sex was a good thing as long as you did it within the bounds of monog-amous, heterosexual marriage, but as many married Chris-tians have discovered, it's difficult to flip a switch and magically stop feeling guilty about sex on your wedding night. When it is so tied up with the fear of hell, sexuality can never truly be enjoyed or celebrated as the gift that it is, inside or outside of marriage. For me, sexuality was not a beloved part of my hu-manness, and certainly not a part of my spirituality. It was a source of shame.

My struggles with sexuality and self-loathing were chal-lenging enough as a straight person, but they paled in comparison to the experiences of my LGBTQ friends raised in the church. I was made to feel shame for my sexual desire, but at least it aligned with heteronormativity. It was sin, but it was "normal" sin. Queer people who are raised in the church are made to feel an extra level of shame. There is no hope of a future wedding night where sex magically becomes acceptable. They're told that the very nature of their desires is disordered and sinful, which means that even if they resist those desires, something is still deeply wrong with them. I thought I needed to stop jerking off or I might go to hell. My poor gay friends thought they were going to hell just for existing. Unsurprisingly, this attack on their basic identity causes many queer people to hate themselves.

Jake, who I mentioned at the beginning of the chapter, is not alone in struggling to accept and celebrate himself. I have heard story after story of evangelical doctrine driving sexual minorities deep into self-loathing. My friend Derek, who was raised in a conservative church and is now a happily married gay man, shared with me about the fear he felt because of who he was attracted to. In youth group, teenage boys were encouraged to "share their struggles" and to "hold each other accountable" for sexual sin. They would talk about the girls they were attracted to or about how they were tempted to look at porn. Even in those moments of confession, Derek didn't feel safe to confess because he knew that his sin would be seen as more deformed than the straight kids'. Derek prayed fervently for God to change him, but it never happened. How could he ever be sure that he was truly "saved," if his sexuality continued to be so sinful? He sat in those confession circles with the flames of hell licking at his imagination.

Perhaps ironically, because of this extra level of fear driving his spirituality, Derek took his faith more seriously than his straight peers did. While Derek's straight brother, Chuck, stopped going to church during high school, Derek threw himself deeper into religion, doing everything he thought he was supposed to do. I've noticed this pattern among my gay friends who were raised in the church. Because they are made to hate themselves even more profoundly than their straight peers, they often work harder than anyone to "fix" themselves spiritually. They double down on the very thing that is destroying their self-image, hoping that if they just go deep enough, what's broken inside them can be healed.

Derek pledged himself to celibacy and spent a year as a missionary. He even attempted conversion therapy, where trained ministry leaders cast demons out of him and tried their damnedest to "pray the gay away." In the end, of course, he was still gay. The only thing they managed to do was to give him even deeper psychological scars.

In a way, all of evangelical Christianity is like conversion therapy. Its message for Derek and for everyone is: "Something is deeply wrong with you, and if it doesn't get fixed, you're going to hell." The evangelical gospel tells us that we have a disease (original sin) and offers us a cure (salvation, prayer, going to church, and so on). Derek drank down as much of that cure as he could, and it only served to give him a *real* problem: self-hatred.

All of this is based on a misdiagnosis. We are not born with a disease. The Bible never says we inherit sin. The first thing God said about humanity was that we are "very good" (Genesis 1:31), and this is never revised. Goodness is intrinsic to our nature. Of course we have the capacity to do evil as well. As God tells Cain, "sin is crouching at your door" (Genesis 4:7). We all make choices that shape the kind of person we become. We can act in ways that disconnect us from God and others, or we can act in ways that lovingly draw us together. But the Bible doesn't say that we inherit sin. We inherit the image of God.

GOOD INSIDE

When we look into the face of a child, our intuition knows this to be true: This child is good inside. Despite this intuitive fact, this is not what I was taught to think about children. I was raised in a household that prioritized immediate obedience to authorities, based on the belief that children are sinners whose behavior needs modification. I remember my parents singing the "obedience song" to me and my siblings:

> *Obedience is the very best way to show that you believe*
> *Doing exactly what the Lord commands, doing it happily*

What I was taught about myself as a child has had impacts on how I treat my own children. Recently, while my parents were visiting, my six-year-old, Remy, was refusing to put on his seat belt because of an issue he was having with a toy. I grew frustrated, because I had already started driving and he still wasn't buckled in. I didn't want to take the time to pull over and address his issue—I just wanted him to listen to me and buckle his seat belt! I began to assert my authority, and Remy continued to resist. My dad, observing the conflict, started singing the obedience song. My brain immediately snapped to an image of myself as a six-year-old, upset and agitated, my parents demanding that I obey them. I pulled over and told my dad that this wasn't an issue of disobedience. Remy wasn't being a "bad kid"; he was just overwhelmed. He didn't need me to scold him; he needed my help. My dad remarked that it was a power struggle for authority: Either my six-year-old had the power, or I did.

I want to acknowledge that many children of fundamentalist parents experienced far worse—my own parents, while holding these beliefs, have always been deeply kind and loving people. But even loving parents can pass on harmful theology. If we believe that all people, including our children, are inherently bad, then the best we can do is use force to get them to do "the right thing." This was the perspective that was ingrained in me, and as a result, it was easy for me to see my kids' emotional distress as rebellion—as evidence of their sin nature. I was often failing to connect with my kids, because in the moments they most needed my comfort and connection, I viewed their behavior as disobedience. But my children are not inherently wicked. They are just children. And if that's true, then maybe I'm not inherently wicked either. As I heard my dad singing the obedience song in the car that day, I realized that I was taught to believe in my own badness and that this toxic belief was leaking out of me onto my children. Our fundamental assumptions about human nature shape how we view ourselves and everyone else.

As I've grappled with these issues in my parenting, I have found "connected parenting" experts to be helpful, not only for practical tips but also for reshaping how I view myself and my children. In her book *Good Inside*, clinical psychologist Dr. Becky Kennedy discusses how believing that our children are either fundamentally bad or fundamentally good changes how we interact with them: "As soon as we tell ourselves, 'Okay, slow down . . . I'm good inside . . . my kid is good inside too . . . ,' we intervene differently than we would if we allowed our frustration and anger to dictate our decisions." Those of us who were raised under the belief that we were born worthy of hell may have a very difficult time changing the way we view our inner natures.

Megan Von Fricken, a therapist specializing in religious

trauma, says, "Children raised in authoritarian religions often enter adulthood feeling 'starved for love' because their
parents consistently prioritized obedience and compliance
over nurture and connection." If your upbringing was anything like mine, you may need to sit with that quote for a
moment. This need for compliant children comes from the
belief that children (and therefore all people) are innately
bad, not innately good.

Because we are taught to see ourselves this way from such
a young age, we continue seeing ourselves this way as adults.
Kennedy points out that "our body's circuitry" is wired when
we are young. "In our early years, our body is learning under
what conditions we receive love and attention and understanding and affection, and under what conditions we get rejected, punished, and left alone. . . . We quickly begin to
embrace whatever gets us love and attention, and shut down
and label as 'bad' any parts that get rejected, criticized, or
invalidated." For example: our sexuality, our gender identity,
our ability to disagree with an authority figure, or our ability
to use our own moral intuition. In conservative forms of
Christianity, these are considered "bad" parts of ourselves,
which flow out of our sin nature. These things may send us
to hell.

Kennedy writes that in order to help her children "to feel
good inside, to feel valuable and lovable and worthy, even
when they struggle," she had to start by "re-accessing my
own goodness. My goodness has always been there." This is
not something I was ever taught to feel about myself, and yet
I find that I can't help but believe this about my own children.

This has not come easily. At first, when my kids misbe-
haved, my instinct was still to punish them in the same ways
that I was once punished. When I refused to give in to that
impulse, my inner child had a visceral response. After all, *I*

was punished for this when I was a child. This isn't fair! "No," I told myself. "You didn't deserve it then, and they don't deserve it now. These are children. They need boundaries, not punishment. These are *my children*. They need a father, not a dictator."

If it's true for them, it's true for me. My children are worthy of love and undeserving of punishment. I am worthy of love and undeserving of punishment. *You* are worthy of love, and undeserving of punishment. This "re-parenting" that I was coaching myself through went far beyond my need to undo the authoritarian parenting style I was trained in. It meant rewiring my relationship with myself and my relationship with God.

I don't blame my parents for their parenting style. They were parenting the best way they knew how. They were not negligent; they were misinformed. They cared deeply about being good parents and read many parenting books, but these Christian parenting books only reinforced this lie: that our children are innately bad. We were taught to believe that we were deserving of punishment—punishment from our parents, punishment from God, and the self-inflicted punishment of shame and self-hatred. But this does not fit with our nature as God's beloved image bearers, and it does not reflect the spirituality of Jesus. It is rooted in fear—in hell.

At some point I had to decide that I wasn't a better parent than God. If I can see the best in my children, even as a flawed human father, then so can God. Choosing to see the best in others is transformative in all our relationships, including the one we have with ourselves. As Richard Rohr says, "I have never met a truly compassionate or loving human being who did not have a foundational and even deep trust in the inherent goodness of human nature." Learning to love ourselves does not make us narcissists. To the contrary,

I have found that people who are gracious and kind to themselves are often more able to extend that grace and kindness to others.

For many of you, this idea of inner goodness may seem to fly in the face of Christian doctrine. Maybe it would be helpful to know that the doctrine of original sin was invented by Augustine of Hippo four hundred years after Jesus lived; it is based on a mistranslation of Romans 5:12 and is not present at all in the Eastern Orthodox church. But, doctrine aside, I want us to consider how this belief in our badness has disconnected us from ourselves and how this has affected our spirituality.

A low view of ourselves made us vulnerable. We were taught to despise ourselves, so we did not learn to listen to ourselves. Believing ourselves to be untrustworthy, we outsourced our spiritual lives to patriarchal authorities. They told us to "trust the Bible" instead of our intuition, and we took their word for what the Bible meant—even though there is no single objectively correct interpretation of what the Bible meant, and our religious leaders often had harmful theological agendas, such as the exclusion of queer people and the subordination of women.

We did not learn how to look for the beauty inside, or listen to the goodness in our inner voice, the wisdom of our intuition. We did not learn how to connect to the best parts of ourselves or how to nurture that inner goodness. The spirituality of hell is deficient because it hurts us and because it is a lie. It disconnects us from ourselves because it is not aligned with the truth of who we are: God's precious image bearers, reflections of divine love. The foundation of a healthy relationship with ourselves is knowing that we are worthy of love.

At his baptism, God spoke these words over Jesus: "This

is my beloved Son; with whom I am well pleased" (Matthew 3:17, ESV). Before Jesus healed anyone, preached a single sermon, or forgave a single person—before he did anything at all—he was called beloved. Christian spirituality may be as simple as learning to live as if those words that were spoken over Jesus are also spoken over us: "You are my beloved child; with you I am well pleased." This belovedness is where a true relationship with God begins.

The gospel—the good news—is that you are already fully loved and accepted. That's the message of grace at the heart of Christianity. You don't have to do anything to be loved. *Not anything at all.* The work is always to *receive* it, to *believe* it. You don't need to "be saved" to be loved. Salvation is just a way of describing the moment we come to know and believe that we are *already* loved, that we have *always been* loved. And our belovedness is not in spite of who we are but simply because we are worthy of love.

But hell makes it very hard to believe in our belovedness. The terrifying consequences of our supposed innate wickedness do not leave room for the possibility that God may actually rejoice over us, exactly as we are. If your spirituality left no room for loving and embracing yourself, and instead only taught you to debase yourself, then I want you to know that you are not alone.

My message to you is the same as my message to Jake, and to Derek, and to my own children, and to myself, because I still need to hear it: You are loved, right now, by God, with a love that has never left you. God never wanted you to hate yourself. God is not going to damn you, especially not for being the way God created you. The loving life that God wants for you cannot begin with self-hatred. God wants you to love yourself with the same love that God desires to flow between every one of God's precious creatures. To love yourself with the same love with which we love our neighbors. To love yourself with the same love that God spoke over Jesus, the beloved Son. To love yourself without feeling the least bit guilty for loving yourself, knowing that it is a good and holy thing to do, because you are worthy of love.

And so is everybody else.

4.

DOGMA, DAMNATION, AND COLONIZATION

*How a Spirituality of
Hell Disconnects Us from Others*

The beginning of love is the will to let those we love be perfectly themselves, the resolution not to twist them to fit our own image.

—Thomas Merton

Oh God, did I hate passing out tracts. Every Thursday, our church would head down into the subway station for tract ministry. Evangelism, baby. I hated it, and I hated myself for hating it. I would stick my arm out, thrusting a gospel tract into someone's hands while trying to avoid eye contact. The truly zealous and effective "soul winners" did a lot more than that. My dad would attempt to start a conversation, the whole point of which was to lead to the zinger question: "If you die today, do you know for sure where you're going?"

Believing that someone is going to hell has an unsurprisingly negative effect on how you view that person. "Damned" is a hell of a category to put someone in (pun intended). If I damn someone in my mind, I cannot experience solidarity with them—we are not all in this together. Our fates are drastically different. We are worlds apart.

The spirituality of hell is fear based, and fear always separates. It is very difficult to be inclusive or accept someone as they are if you believe that who they are will result in eternal damnation. If that's the case, you are required to change them, to save them. Accepting them would actually mean giving up on them; it would be giving them over to their unthinkably awful fate.

I'll remind you once again that Jesus tells us that the greatest commandment is to love God, and that the second, which is equally important, is to love our neighbors as ourselves.

The doctrine of hell makes this impossible because, just as it disconnects us from God and from ourselves, hell disconnects us from our neighbors.

OUR MISSION FIELD

If you interviewed just about any evangelical pastor (and plenty of nonevangelical pastors) in America and asked them what the mission of their church was, they would ultimately admit that it was to get as many people as possible to convert to Christianity. They probably wouldn't say it so bluntly, at least not at first. They might start by saying they exist "to make Jesus famous" or even something nice like "to spread the love of God." But if you drilled down to what they meant by that, they would ultimately have to admit that it was all about conversion. It has to be! Hell is too important for it to be otherwise.

Now, there are some evangelical churches and leaders who believe that social justice and good works are an important part of our calling as Christians. However, whenever this viewpoint starts to gain traction, the larger evangelical institution takes pains to shut it down. For example, conservative pastors Kevin DeYoung and Greg Gilbert wrote the popular book *What Is the Mission of the Church?* precisely in order to quash the creeping popularity of social justice in the church and insist that the mission of the church should be primarily focused on saving souls. As long as hell is a part of their gospel story, the danger of hell will always be far greater than the danger of injustice in this world. This is why although many evangelical churches will gesture toward justice-related issues, they will struggle to make it anything more than window dressing.

When I first became an evangelical pastor, one of the

most popular buzzwords was *missional*. Everything we did needed to be missional, and everywhere we went, we were supposed to be "on mission." Many of these missional churches even conducted training events for how to live on mission. I remember one pastor sharing ideas such as throwing a neighborhood block party, holding a free yard sale, or paying for a stranger's gas at the gas station. But the purpose of these acts of kindness was not purely to spread love. The purpose was to convert nonbelievers into believers. Evangelicals learned the holy art of the bait and switch. Our primary job as Christians was conversion. How could it not be?

But if our primary job was to see our neighbors get saved, then they were not really our neighbors; they were our mission field. We were carrying the only message of salvation. They *needed* us. This was not a mutual relationship, which requires that both parties respect each other and contribute meaningfully to the relationship. If I believe that you're going to burn for eternity unless you listen to me and agree with me, then you are my *project*, not my friend. I don't need to have curiosity or listen to you. I need to save you. This creates a sense of superiority and alienation.

Hell-based theology feeds a colonizer mentality in which we believe the world "out there" is lost and broken but *we* have the answers to fix it. The *others* are going to hell for being wrong—they need our system of faith and our way of life. They need to be saved. This perverse logic has justified unimaginable cruelty throughout history, from the genocide of Indigenous people to the enslavement of African people. The doctrine of hell provided perfect theological cover for this colonization and allowed white Christians to baptize their savagery as holy. After all, what was the loss of land, culture, and life compared to the urgency of saving souls from eternal torment?

Hell gave colonizers spiritual justification for white supremacy. White Christians positioned themselves as the gate-
keepers of heaven and hell, the arbiters of who was "saved"
and who was "lost." White culture, white interpretation of
scripture, and white ways of worship were superior, and everyone else's spirituality was dismissed as primitive, pagan, and
headed for eternal damnation. In this sense, white supremacy
has historically been inseparable from Christian supremacy
and exclusivism. There may be nothing more damaging to our
connectedness with one another than a colonizing, supremacist mentality undergirded by hell theology.

Christian supremacy is not just a global problem. Growing up, I experienced this alienation firsthand, in my own
family. My dad came to his fundamentalist faith as an adult,
and the rest of his family did not believe like we did. This was
a constant topic of discussion and prayer. As a child, I was
unaware of the way Dad's brothers and sisters viewed our
fundamentalist family. I was only aware of how we viewed
them, and that was as unbelievers.

My dad's older brother was an audio engineer who often
hosted holiday parties in his Manhattan apartment. David
was his given name, but in high school he started going by
Rex, short for Recker, our surname. This seemed eminently
cool to me as a child (and later to my son, who at six years old
started demanding we call him Rex too). Rex and his wife,
Renee, had no kids, but they did have several cats, modern
furniture, music that I wasn't ordinarily allowed to listen to,
and wine that they drank from fancy glasses. I looked up to
Rex—but I also believed he was a sinner, headed for hell. We
would pray for Rex at night before bed, along with our other
unsaved family members. We prayed that they would believe
in Jesus so that they could go to heaven when they died.

On the way to Christmas parties at Rex's in our station

wagon, my parents would prepare us. "Kids," my dad would say over his shoulder to my sister and me in his father/pastor voice, "you know my family doesn't know the Lord, so they're going to be drinking, probably using the Lord's name in vain. In fact, Debbie, can you say a prayer right now for God's peace in our midst this evening?"

Almost every drive began with a prayer. "Yes, Lord!" my mom would begin. "We KNOW that you will be with us tonight as we go visit Matthew's precious family. Please open their hearts, Lord! Would you help us, Lord, to be LIGHTS, to know how to speak with them, Lord. Give us wisdom! In Jesus's name, amen."

On the drive home, we would pray again, recapping the evening's various sins and asking once more for our family members' salvation. I still admire my parents' pure faith in a God who heard our prayers, a God who was always present with us and who would act in love for us. But our faith in God actually became an enemy of love, because we saw other people as separate from us and from God.

My dad had a vivid painting of heaven and hell over his dresser, to remind him of what mattered most.* Every morning as he got ready, he was confronted with eternity. Rescuing people from hell. Nothing mattered more. I used to feel guilt at how little desire I had to evangelize, compared to my dad. I assumed this made him a more spiritual person than I was.

I can see now that my guilt was misplaced—almost all the characteristics of spirituality that I was taught to admire and emulate were actually negative traits. When hell is at the center of our spirituality, it creates a malformed version of spiritual maturity. In that view, a mature, spiritual Christian can

---

* *The Bridge*, by William Ressler, if you'd like to google it. It's quite horrifying.

be abrasive, judgmental, divisive, and pushy. Thankfully, unlike many conservative Christians I have encountered, my dad has the ability to be kind to people who disagree with him, and for that I am very grateful. And yet, there was a distance in our relationship with our extended family. We believed that they were lost and we were saved. This gave us an alienating false superiority: We were the ones who had the truth. They were objects of our prayer; they were a mission field.

I will never forget the last time my Uncle Rex ever visited the fundamentalist church my dad pastored in New York City. Rex lived in midtown Manhattan, just a few neighborhoods over, but he never came, despite constant invitations. One year, my dad invited Dr. Bob Jones III (yes, the same Dr. Bob whose university I would go on to attend) as a special guest speaker. He told Rex how much it would mean to him for Rex to show up, and Rex obliged. On the drive to church that morning, there was an extra element of pleading in our prayers.

The title of Dr. Bob's sermon, I will never forget, was "How Hot Is Hell." I squirmed anxiously in my chair, thinking of how this sermon would hit Rex. It was a familiar feeling. When hell came up in a sermon, I would find myself thinking of how these condemnations were making people feel. I knew that I was supposed to be glad that they were hearing "the truth," but instead I wanted to disappear.

At the end of the service, Rex left politely but immediately. As far as I am aware, he never came again. On the way home, my dad reflected on how even though it was a hard word, at least Rex got to hear the truth. None of this felt good to me at the time, but I assumed that the deficiency was in myself. If hell was real—and my entire system of belief insisted that it was—then Dr. Bob's sermon was appropriate and necessary. People needed to be warned.

I have a lot of sympathy for the way my dad believes that many of his dearest family members are going to hell. In the moments when his rigid beliefs are hurting our relationship, I try to remember how that must feel. It's a hell of a thing to believe. When someone who believes in hell says or does something that makes me feel rejected, I try to remind myself that from the vantage point of their beliefs, they're probably trying to love me. Unfortunately, nothing fucks up love like hell.

JESUS'S MISSION FIELD

Jesus also had a mission field. However, Jesus's mission had exactly the opposite effect of the conversion-obsessed mission of white evangelical Christianity. Where this hell-fueled mission led to division, exclusion, and colonization, Jesus's mission brought connection and liberation. In Luke 4:18, Jesus launches his ministry by publicly proclaiming, "The Spirit of the Lord is on me, because he has anointed me to proclaim good news to the poor."

When we follow Jesus on his mission of good news to the poor, we see that "the poor" include not only the materially poor but also socially excluded people like prostitutes, lepers, and tax collectors (who were widely despised at the time because they collected taxes from their fellow Jews to pay the occupying Roman Empire). In one famous story, Jesus specifically seeks out and dines with a tax collector named Zacchaeus, and announces that he "came to seek and to save the lost" (Luke 19:10). Many Christians will quote that verse to tell people that they are lost and therefore need to be saved.

But Jesus did not tell people they were lost. Jesus identified people who society labeled as lost, or who considered themselves lost, *and he included them.*

Jesus is never the one telling people they are lost. Jesus is always the one welcoming them home.

Jesus's inclusiveness bothered certain religious authorities, so Jesus explains what he's up to by telling stories of reconciliation—of the recovery of lost things and lost people. In Luke 15, Jesus tells three parables about lost things being found. The way these stories are introduced tells us exactly what their purpose is: "Now the tax collectors and sinners were all gathering around to hear Jesus. But the Pharisees and the teachers of the law muttered, 'This man welcomes sinners and eats with them.' Then Jesus told them this parable" (Luke 15:1–3).

The most famous of the stories Jesus then tells is commonly called the parable of the prodigal son. This story is about two brothers. The younger brother disgraces their father by taking his inheritance early, leaving home, and immediately wasting all his money on "wild living" (Luke 15:13). Meanwhile, the older brother stays at home working for their father, as he is expected to do. At the end of the story, the wandering son, penniless and desperate, returns home to beg for mercy, and the father throws a great feast for him. He doesn't bring up the son's offense or demand an apology. He just invites him into a celebration. The older brother, who had done what he was supposed to do all along, begins to pout that his younger brother gets a feast while he doesn't. Scandalized by his father's forgiveness, he refuses to join in on the party.

With this story, Jesus was pointing out that many religious authorities, with their dogma and their certitude, were missing out on the inclusive work of grace that Jesus was up to. They were gatekeeping God. In Jesus's stories, God is always hosting feasts, and everyone is always invited—but not everybody chooses to show up. There are always people, like the stubborn older brother, who are unwilling to get in on the party because of who else is inside. The lesson is simple: God includes everyone, and we only exclude ourselves. And the way that we exclude ourselves is through our insistence on excluding others.

Connection with God and others is a feast of love. It's a joy we were made for and one that is always available to us, but it takes an act of opening our hearts. It means recognizing that the party God is throwing is not just for *people like me* or *people who believe like me*. It's for everybody. As Richard Rohr has said, "The only thing Jesus excluded was exclusion itself." It is a great tragedy that Christians took that message of scandalous inclusion and mutated it into a story about needing to convert people.

In another story Jesus told, known as the parable of the good Samaritan, a Jewish man is robbed, beaten, and left for dead at the side of the road. After being passed over by several people of his own nationality and religion, he is rescued and bandaged up by a Samaritan—a despised heretic in the eyes of Jewish people at the time. Samaritans' theology was considered wrong. They didn't worship in the right way or at the right temple. If there was such a thing as hell, it was for Samaritans. And yet, the wounded man is saved by this supposed unbeliever. The story does not mention the Samaritan being forgiven of his sins, being born again, or being converted to the right religion. It is the "unbeliever" who *brings* salvation in this story. The heretic isn't saved—*he is the savior.*

Many evangelicals are so busy trying to save their neighbor from hell, they miss out on the salvation they could receive *from* their neighbor. For example, by assuming that queer people are destined for hell, conservative Christians have missed the opportunity to learn from their queer brothers and sisters. Having experienced exclusion and marginalization, queer people have an incredible capacity for compassion, inclusion, and personal transformation. They could teach the church so much. Yet instead of sitting at their feet and learning from them, the church has mostly excluded and wounded them.

Similarly, colonizers' focus on "saving" Indigenous people blinded them to the profound spiritual wisdom Indigenous cultures held. The deep understanding of our connection to the land and the practices of communal care in many Indigenous cultures could have enriched Christian spirituality immensely. Instead, colonizers destroyed these traditions in the name of "salvation," impoverishing both Indigenous communities and their own spiritual understanding. It is not these communities that needed to be saved from hell by the church. In many ways, it is the church that needs to be saved by the very people it has arrogantly neglected—the people the church assumed needed salvation.

Salvation is not about choosing the right theological beliefs to avoid hell. It's about recognizing the goodness and divinity in the despised "other" and joining in on the party God is throwing, where everybody is invited. Jesus never tells people they need to change their doctrine or convert to another religion in order to be saved from hell. Jesus doesn't defend *theology*, he defends the *humanity* of the vulnerable and the marginal. Jesus doesn't explain the one correct statement of faith to his disciples; he meets real human needs, while calling out religious leaders for the hypocrisy of caring more about dogma than justice and mercy.

Hell is not a good Christian doctrine because it makes it impossible to show up in relationships with others like Jesus did. The spirituality of hell excludes and others people; Jesus includes the "other" and shows us that we are all more similar than we thought. We are connected, whether we are aware of it or not. Refusing to see this—that is hell. The true hell is exclusion and denying our shared belovedness. It is living in the delusion of superiority and separation. It is refusing to join the banquet where *everyone is invited*.

A SPIRITUALITY WITHOUT PUNISHMENT

Recently, I posted a question on Instagram: "What would be different about your spirituality if there was no punishment in God?" Take a moment to consider how you would answer that question for yourself. Here are some of the replies I received:

I wouldn't be as scared of a relationship with God.

I would be out to my parents.

I would allow myself space to question and explore without fear of becoming polluted by "the world."

I would never have made being timid an intrinsic part of my personality.

I would love myself sooner and critique myself less.

Less shame and confusion. Less pressure to parent with punishment.

I think there would be more joy attached to it rather than a gut feeling that I don't measure up.

I wouldn't feel the pressure to evangelize, I could just be myself and love people.

I would stop feeling guilty about not being an overseas missionary.

I would stop overthinking "mistakes," and start thinking more about how to make the world a better place.

I would have found that I can be gay and Christian and not have tried to end my life.

I would feel a lot lighter, and more true. Not full of shame. It would feel like Eden.

Freeeeeeeedom!!

We were made for this kind of love—love for God, others, and ourselves—but for many of us, a spirituality of hell stands in our way. Before we can embrace a Christian spirituality of love, we will have to deconstruct the harmful doctrine of hell. In the next section, we will look deeply at the so-called facts undergirding the doctrine of hell, especially what the Bible has to say. But first, we are going to briefly look at why the doctrine of hell remains so prevalent in so many churches, despite the harm it causes. In the next chapter, we'll look at how very human power dynamics keep us from challenging the exclusionary, punishing theology that disconnects us from the love we were made for.

Part II

Deconstructing Hell

5.

UNDER PRESSURE

Deconstructing the Power Dynamics of Hell

The evangelical world is tightly networked, and those networks have long policed the borders of "acceptable" evangelical identity.

—Kristin Kobes Du Mez

After I graduated from Bob Jones University, I joined the Marine Corps as an officer and was stationed in coastal North Carolina. This was my first time living outside the fundamentalist restrictions of either my parents or Bob Jones, and I started attending a growing church with more modern sensibilities, one where the pastors could have tattoos and drink the occasional beer. After years of legalistic spirituality and dusty hymns with organ accompaniment, this mainstream evangelical church, with its high-quality graphic design, moody stage lighting, and outward emphasis on grace, was a breath of fresh air.

When I got out of the Marine Corps after a tour in Afghanistan, I eagerly threw myself into evangelical ministry. Doug, the lead pastor of my church, who had tattoos and a long *Duck Dynasty*–style beard, sat me down and asked if I would consider joining them in planting a new church location in an old chapel by the sea. I felt I had finally found my calling. However, after a couple years in pastoral ministry, I realized I was still deeply disturbed by the doctrine of hell. We didn't broadcast it like the fundamentalists, but it became clearer and clearer to me that it undergirded all of our theology.

So I was delighted when, about five years after becoming a pastor, I discovered through my personal study that the Bible did not demand belief in eternal conscious torment. I felt liberated—but I also felt confused and betrayed. Why was the church as I knew it so obsessed with hell? Why would anyone choose to believe something so traumatic and spiritually harmful if the text didn't require it? Were respected evangelical leaders like Tim Keller and Don Carson unaware of the dismal biblical support for hell, or did they just not care? It was a mind-fuck for me. Grappling with these questions undermined my confidence in the entire evangelical system. *What else weren't they telling me?*

In the next chapter, we'll deconstruct hell by looking at what the Bible says and seeing that it doesn't match what so many of us have been taught. But first, I want to examine the top-down systemic pressure in Christianity, particularly in evangelicalism, that makes hell a very difficult doctrine to break up with, whether you're a pastor or a parishioner. To deconstruct hell, you will have to contend with much more than the text, because hell isn't just maintained by biblical interpretation—it's upheld by a complex web of institutional pressure, financial incentives, and career consequences. The whole system demands hell.

THE SYSTEM PROTECTS ITSELF

Within any conservative Christian institution, there are unspoken rules about which theological ideas can be questioned and which cannot. Evangelicals often refer to these as *open-handed* and *closed-handed* issues. Open-handed issues are things you can freely disagree on, like Bible translations or Communion practices; if you prefer the New International Version of the Bible but your pastor prefers the English Standard Version, you will still be considered a Christian and welcomed into the evangelical church. Closed-handed issues are the nonnegotiables, like Jesus's divinity. You could go to church every Sunday and fully believe in God, but if you think that Jesus was merely a wise spiritual leader rather than a part of the Holy Trinity, evangelicalism would not consider you Christian, and any discussion of your views would be quickly and forcefully shut down.

This may seem simple enough in theory, but in practice, the lines can be quite arbitrary. In centuries past, people were burned at the stake over differences in Communion and baptism that are now considered open-handed. And despite the Bible saying very little about gender and sexuality, affirming stances on the LGBTQ community are now considered big-ticket closed-handed issues that can get you exiled from the evangelical world.

Hell is an issue that has been placed firmly in the "closed hand." Just look at what happened to Rob Bell.

Bell, the founding pastor of Mars Hill Bible Church in Grandville, Michigan, had long had a reputation for being on the edge of what was acceptable in evangelical circles. He wrote liberal-leaning books with titles like *Velvet Elvis* and *Sex God*, but his church was wildly popular and he remained in evangelicalism's good graces overall. Then, in 2011, he published *Love Wins: A Book About Heaven, Hell, and the Fate of Every Person Who Ever Lived*, in which he dared to question the traditional view of hell and suggested that all people would be ultimately reconciled to God. The book was a hit with readers; it sold thousands and thousands of copies, earning itself a spot on the *New York Times* bestseller list. But for the evangelical establishment, it was quite literally heresy.

It's a good book. I know, because I recently read it, more than a decade after its publication. You may be wondering: Why would a Bible nerd with a thirst for knowledge and an interest in the afterlife spend ten-plus years avoiding a blockbuster book that explores a crucially important theological topic? Because of a John Piper tweet, of course. In response to *Love Wins*, Piper, the popular pastor and cofounder of the influential evangelical website The Gospel Coalition, tweeted three simple words: "Farewell Rob Bell."

Everyone in the evangelical world knew exactly what Piper's tweet meant. Bell was no longer one of us. It was also a warning to anyone who might be considering challenging the party line on the doctrine of hell: *Don't you dare.* You see, for all their bemoaning of "cancel culture," nobody knows how to execute swift judgment on dissenting opinions quite like evangelicals. After the controversy of *Love Wins*, all of Bell's books were removed from the shelves in evangelical bookstores, and he was forced to step down as pastor of Mars Hill. As a young pastor at the time, I got the message loud and clear. "Farewell Rob Bell" could easily become "Farewell Brian Recker." Questioning hell would get me branded a "liberal compromiser" who didn't take the Bible seriously. That would mean losing my career, my community—everything.

This is how conservative institutions enforce particular interpretations of key doctrines from the top down. When someone's salary and status in a community are tied to maintaining certain beliefs and boundaries, that person will find it very difficult to question those beliefs. Quite ironically, though a pastor or professional theologian may have a great deal more formal education than the average churchgoer, they may be far *less* objective when it comes to honestly evaluating a theological position.

Rob Bell is far from the only person to experience the consequences of changing his mind on key evangelical doctrines like hell. The Bible scholar Pete Enns wrote of the resistance he experienced in his theological evolution on such doctrines, especially when it came to disappointing "friends and family, along with ecclesiastical authorities—and those who signed my paychecks." Following his conscience and being honest about the Bible ultimately made him, in his words, "an outsider in my own community, a suspicious character, a rebel, one who could not be trusted to speak of God, lend money to, or watch your pets." Enns went on to lose his high-ranking tenured seminary position for his changing views.*

Carlton Pearson, a hugely influential Pentecostal preacher who grew a megachurch of six thousand people, also famously changed his mind about the existence of hell in the early 2000s. He had been at the top of his denomination: a bishop, a sought-after conference speaker, a member of George W. Bush's faith counsel, and a respected mentor to T.D. Jakes, one of the most influential prominent Black pastors in America. But when Pearson changed his mind about hell, he lost everything. His pastoral team quit, and there was "a mass exodus" from his church. His offerings dwindled, and staff had to be let go as his church of six thousand condensed to two hundred. Pearson was uninvited from conferences and officially declared a heretic by the Joint College of African American Pentecostal Bishops. Even his mentee T.D. Jakes distanced himself, calling Pearson's theology "wrong, false, misleading."

It is incredibly rare for leaders like Bell, Enns, and Pearson to change their minds on hell, not because the doctrine of hell is so solid *but because they have so much to lose.* The way that evangelicals interpret the "hell passages" in the Bible is inseparable from the institutional pressure that enforces those interpretations.

And when this pressure to toe the line on hell affects

---

* Enns now runs *The Bible for Normal People,* a wonderful podcast and online resource that brings progressive Bible scholarship to popular audiences.

pastors and theologians, it inevitably trickles down to everyone. Regular Christians, who came to faith through a heaven-or-hell choice, would understandably be very confused if their pastor suddenly shifted on hell, which helps create a mutually reinforcing system. Parishioners believe in a spirituality of hell because they receive it from their pastors, and pastors are unable to change their interpretation of hell because their parishioners believe in it. The average churchgoer starting to question the existence of hell would be afraid to voice their doubts lest they be reprimanded by church leadership; likewise, a pastor questioning the existence of hell would be afraid to voice their doubts lest their flock turn on them, either by emptying the pews or by getting the pastor removed altogether.

Not only that, but as we will discuss in the second half of this book, hell is so deeply woven into the Christian narrative that most believers would struggle to extract it from their faith, even if they wanted to. Like trying to operate on a cancer that has spread to vital organs, ripping out hell threatens to tear the whole Christian faith to shreds.

To attack a closed-hand doctrine like hell is to attack the whole system, which is almost impossible to do. The system is built to protect itself.

COMING OUT AGAINST HELL

When I finally began to deconstruct hell, I was still a pastor under these institutional pressures. I saw how weak the biblical support was for the traditional position of eternal conscious torment, but as an evangelical, I knew that a *universalist* position—believing that all people will ultimately be reconciled to God, no matter what—would be a bridge too far. So my first step was to take an *annihilationist* position, which is the belief that "unsaved" people will be destroyed rather than suffer eternally. For annihilationists, believers go to heaven, and everyone else just stops existing.

I knew that even this middle-ground position could make waves. I had double-checked our church's statement of faith, and sure enough, there was a line about those who reject Jesus suffering for eternity in hell. I no longer believed this, and my integrity did not permit me to ignore that. As a multisite pastor, I had some autonomy, but I was accountable to the larger elder team, which was made up of elders at all four of our sites. I knew I would have to tell the lead pastor, Doug, about the conclusion I had come to. Having heard the stories of pastors and teachers who had been forced out of their evangelical ministries for dissenting against evangelical orthodoxy, I prepared myself for the worst, but I knew I couldn't live with myself if I didn't speak out.

After I'd word-vomited out my new position, Doug leaned in with an intense look of concern, his long beard wagging at me. "So, you don't believe that unbelievers go to hell."

"Correct," I said.

"But you do believe they're annihilated?"

"Right. I believe that is a more biblical position."

"Okay. So . . ." He paused. "So you still think *something bad* is going to happen to them, right?"

Even before he asked that question, I knew that this would be his concern. The threat of punishment was foundational to our theology. "Something bad" had to happen to "them." Why be a Christian if there was no punishment for non-Christians?

Plenty of evangelical leaders would have been willing to fire me for that. To his credit, Doug was satisfied to make room for multiple views of hell, as long as there was a threat of *some* kind of punishment for unbelief.

And so, with the understanding that my new view was appropriately punishing, we transitioned to a communication plan. Should anyone know about my change in position? I wanted to tell people, because I knew there were probably others in the church who struggled with the doctrine of hell, and the simple awareness that other views were *possible* could be a lifeline to their faith. Doug saw where I was coming from, but he knew as well as I did how reactive evangelical churchgoers could be. For every person who would be excited about a less severe view of hell, there would be several more accusing us of "going soft" on the hard truths of scripture. Not only that, but the people most likely to feel that way would be the older wealthy conservatives whose giving kept the church afloat. Doug didn't say all of that out loud, but he didn't have to. I knew what the fallout was likely to be.

We decided to just keep it quiet for the time being. Doug would think about it and figure out what to do. But the subject never came up again. A few years later, I stepped down from pastoring completely.

When I finally stepped down, it wasn't directly because of my beliefs about hell. Mostly it was because I couldn't stomach evangelicalism's embrace of Donald Trump and Christian nationalism. But once I was no longer obligated to buy into the beliefs mandated by the church's power structure, I was shocked at how quickly I changed my mind on other issues, such as LGBTQ affirmation. I abandoned annihilationism and became a universalist, which is just as well supported in scripture, and fits far better with the loving nature of God, but would have been out-of-bounds for an evangelical pastor.

While I was a pastor, I could never truly evaluate any of these beliefs on the merits. When I studied any of these hotbutton issues, I always did it with the knowledge in the back of my mind that if I were to change my view, I would lose my salary, my reputation, and my entire relational network, which revolved around the group of evangelical churches I was a part of. It would mean being rejected by my community, being pitied or reviled as someone who had fallen away. I would join my Uncle Rex as the subject of prayer requests.

And sure enough, the consequences were swift. When I publicly announced my support for same-sex relationships, my old church took down my eight years of sermons from their church website. It wasn't enough that I had quit; I had to be scrubbed from the record completely. It was painful, but I had come to a place of peace, knowing that my freedom was worth that rejection. I was merely joining the countless groups who had already been excluded or marginalized in our institutions. As a straight white man, I had experienced incredible privilege in the evangelical system. The leadership pipeline and ministry opportunities were built to platform voices like mine. Many others—women, queer people, and people of color—would never have had access to that platform in the first place. Leaving those institutions behind was costly, but it has freed me to be myself and to steward whatever influence I still have to include the people that evangelicalism's rigid system excluded.

BIASED THEN, BIASED NOW

I have recounted my journey out of the traditional view of hell to give you an idea of just how many obstacles there are to shifting the conversation. If you're reading this, you might be facing some of the same obstacles, and you know how much it could cost you to uproot the concept of punishment from your faith. Although I'm somewhat embarrassed at the way material and relational pressures slanted my views while I was a pastor, I'm also proud of myself for taking the steps to get out from under them. Some things are only obvious in hindsight.

But the truth is that we all have biases. We all approach the Bible with "interpretive lenses" that color how we read and understand the text. The best we can do is be aware of the lenses we are wearing and the biases we are carrying. I love how the late Rachel Held Evans describes reading the Bible:

> *If you are looking for Bible verses with which to support slavery, you will find them. If you are looking for verses with which to abolish slavery, you will find them. If you are looking for verses with which to oppress women, you will find them. If you are looking for verses with which to liberate or honor women, you will find them. If you are looking for reasons to wage war, you will find them. If you are looking for reasons to promote peace, you will find them. If you are looking for an outdated and irrelevant ancient text, you will find it. If you are looking for truth, believe me, you will find it. This is why there are times when the most instructive question to bring to the text is not what does it say?, but what am I looking for?*

If you are looking for hell, you will find it, but as we will see in the next chapter, there is a better and more accurate way to read the text. Most conservative pastors are biased toward a punishing interpretation of the text—by their upbringing, by their culture, by the same institutional pressures that I was under as a pastor. Yet they remain completely oblivious of their bias, oblivious of the ways that they are pressured to conform to evangelical dogma on hell.

I am also biased. I read and interpret the Bible with the assumption—the bias—that "God is love" (1 John 4:8). I am

biased against hell, because I can see the harm and disconnection this doctrine causes. I believe I am biased by my
humanity.

Does this mean that I am forced to read the Bible dishon-
estly or twist scriptures that clearly describe hell to fit my personal narrative? No, I do not believe it does. The biblical data
on hell is messy, complicated, and inconsistent. Although you
can find hell if you're looking for it, it is actually very easy to
read the Bible as a faithful Christian and reject the concept
of hell, because the concept of hell is not clearly taught in
the Bible.

Let's talk about that.

6.

HELL ON EARTH

What the Bible Really Says About Hell

I do in fact believe in hell, though only in the sense of a profound and imprisoning misery that we impose upon ourselves by rejecting the love that alone can set us free.

—David Bentley Hart

Hell is real, but it's not a place. Hell is a metaphor, and as a metaphor, it's as real as anything. In fact, some of us may be there right now. Metaphors can be very real when they point to a deeper truth. The evil in this world is so vast, so terrible, so impossible to wrap our minds around that in order to capture it, we need a word weighted with eternity. A word like *hell*.

But the Bible doesn't actually talk about hell, at least not in the way we use that word. It's a lot more complicated than that. In this chapter, we'll take a close look at what the Bible really says about hell, from the meaning of the original Hebrew and Greek terms we translate as *hell*, to the contemporary context of various pieces of biblical imagery, to the way Jesus's audience would have interpreted his words. As you'll see, despite what so many of us have been taught, the Bible does not lay out a clear doctrine about hell and who ends up there, but it does give us a provocative metaphor. When we clear away the misinformation and listen to what this metaphor actually means, we will hear a warning that is just as relevant for our world as it was for the world of Jesus.

BIBLE THUMPING

There is no word for hell in the Bible, not really. There are a few words that are *translated into English* as "hell," but not a single one of them actually means hell in the way we think about it.

The first is the Hebrew word *Sheol*, which appears several times throughout the Old Testament, or Hebrew Bible. Depending on the translation you're reading, you might see Sheol translated as "hell" in some verses, but you'll probably also see it translated as "the grave" or just kept untranslated as the proper noun Sheol. Sheol is often used simply as a metaphor for *death*—an evocative way to describe the mystery we're all headed toward. At times it also seems to describe an actual underworld, but it is certainly never spoken of as a place of suffering and punishment. Everybody went there when they died, not just bad people. Righteous figures like Jacob the patriarch and Job spoke of how they'd one day inevitably go down to Sheol—down to the grave—just like everyone else.*

When the Hebrew Bible was first translated into Greek, in the third century BCE, the word Sheol was rendered as *Hades*, a word you might recognize from Greek mythology. This doesn't mean that all of a sudden the Hebrew Bible endorsed the ancient Greek conception of an underworld ruled by the god of the dead—it just means Greek-speaking translators used the closest word they had to Sheol, which was *Hades*. The New Testament, which was originally written in Greek, also uses the word Hades in various places where the Old Testament would have used Sheol. It is a way of describing death or the grave and does not necessarily imply punishment.

Tartarus, another word from Greek mythology, appears once in the New Testament as well, but it does *not* refer to hell in the sense of a place where sinners are tormented. Rather,

---

* In Genesis 37:35 and Job 17:13, respectively.

in 2 Peter 2:4, the text borrows this term for the pit that imprisoned the Titans and uses it to describe a holding place for fallen angels awaiting judgment. (Yes, you're allowed to think this is weird—the Bible is a strange book.)

We often translate the words *Hades* and *Tartarus* into English as "hell"—a word, by the way, that gets its name from Hel, the realm of the dead described in Norse mythology. But just as we don't assume these words indicate that New Testament authors believed in ancient Greek (or Norse) notions of the afterlife, nor should we assume they indicate belief in our modern notion of hell. These are issues of translation that we have mistaken for issues of doctrine.

The last and perhaps most interesting word that is translated as "hell" in the New Testament is *Gehenna*. This is a place of judgment described by Jesus, but it is not a fiery pit— the word literally means "the Valley of Hinnom," which was a real-ass valley, right outside the gates of Jerusalem.

I'll come back to this in just a moment, but for now I want to note that despite this plethora of terms, hell actually doesn't come up very often in the New Testament. The apostle Paul doesn't mention hell a single time; if the entire point of Christianity is avoiding hell, this seems like an odd oversight for the person who wrote over half of the New Testament! One would think that the potential for never-ending torment would be worth mentioning.

So what *is* the biblical basis for the idea of hell? Surely it has to come from *somewhere* in the Bible, right? Well, sort of. The doctrine of hell primarily comes from one or two verses in the book of Revelation. In case you're unfamiliar, Revelation is highly metaphorical. It is filled with what scholars call *apocalyptic hyperbole*, which means the author is using fantastical images to make a point, but we aren't supposed to take those images as literal. This is the book that talks about the four horsemen, the number of the beast, and so on and so forth. Very bad biblical interpretation has taken these hyper-stylized symbolic images and not only made them literal but also *read those images back into the rest of the Bible.*

As any scholar will tell you, that's not how you're supposed to read the book of Revelation! In fact, theologian David Bentley Hart believes it is "a supremely foolish enterprise for anyone to attempt to extract so much as a single clear and unarguable doctrine regarding anything at all" from the book of Revelation. But of course that hasn't stopped some Christians from using these stupefying images to map out a detailed timeline of the end of the world and the fate of our souls.

So, with that in mind, here it is, the only image in the entire Bible of people being thrown into everlasting torment. If it were not for this one verse in the book of Revelation, the doctrine of hell would probably not exist:

> *And the smoke of their torment goes up forever and ever, and they have no rest, day or night, these worshipers of the beast and its image, and whoever receives the mark of its name.*
>
> Revelation 14:11, ESV

I will grant that, at first glance, that sounds a hell of a lot like hell! If you take this image of torment and project it onto other statements in the Bible, you can see how the myth of hell began to take shape. But is this verse really describing hell?

First of all, it doesn't actually say that anyone will be tormented forever—it's the *smoke* that lasts forever, not the torment itself. And in apocalyptic hyperbole, smoke rising up is commonly used as a symbol of *historical destruction,* especially for the destruction of a city or nation. For example, this passage in Revelation sounds an awful lot like Isaiah's description of the destruction of Edom:

> *And the streams of Edom shall be turned into pitch . . .*
> *Night and day it shall not be quenched;*
> *its smoke shall go up forever.*
>
> Isaiah 34:9–10, ESV

Despite Isaiah's announcement, the ancient kingdom of Edom did not burn forever. Its inhabitants were not tormented in flames for eternity. And Isaiah didn't actually expect them to; this is hyperbole intentionally being used to make a point. Yes, Edom was destroyed by enemy nations, but people eventually returned to the land and rebuilt, as people always do. That doesn't mean the Bible is "untrue"— it just means that's how apocalyptic hyperbole works. Isaiah is communicating God's verdict on Edom, *in history*. They did evil in God's sight, and God brought *historical judgment* upon them—not burning in the afterlife.

The book of Revelation is the same. Despite the conspiracy theories you may have been told about "the mark of the beast," it's not about a barcode or microchip. Most scholars believe that the famous number 666 is referring to the Roman Emperor Nero. Hebrew numerology, called *gematria,* assigns each Hebrew letter a number, and the letters in "Nero Caesar" in Hebrew add up to 666. If no one has ever told you this, I'm sorry, because biblical scholars have been aware of this for quite some time. Revelation is not about hell or the end of the world; it's about God bringing judgment on the Roman Empire, just like God brought judgment on Edom.

Think of it a bit like a political cartoon, using symbolic details to make a point. When we see a talking elephant in a newspaper comic, we know it refers to the Republican Party, not a living African land mammal that has the power of speech. Likewise, Revelation has multiheaded dragons, locusts with human faces, and six-winged creatures covered in eyes to represent various political and historical entities. Most people recognize all of these things as metaphors, but for some reason they don't apply the same logic to the passages that sound like they're describing hell! The simple truth is that Revelation is not talking about people in general suffering for eternity. It's talking about the oppressive Roman Empire experiencing the historical consequences of their violence.

HELL, ACCORDING TO JESUS

"Okay," you might say, "but that's the book of Revelation. Even if that's just a metaphor, what's truly important is what *Jesus* said about hell." Well, Jesus talked about hell in a similar way to Revelation: as a metaphor for a group of people experiencing the historical consequences of their violence. But the metaphor Jesus used was not a multiheaded dragon; it was Gehenna.

If you've ever heard a sermon about hell, you've probably heard a preacher say something like, "Jesus talks about hell more than anybody." This is quite misleading. What Jesus actually talks about more than anybody is Gehenna. If Gehenna is referring to hell, then Jesus spoke about it more than anyone, but if Gehenna is not referring to hell, *then Jesus didn't really speak about hell at all.*

Gehenna, or Ge Ben-Hinnom in Hebrew, is a valley, just south of the city gates of Jerusalem at the time of Jesus. Everyone Jesus was talking to knew what it was and where it was, the same as if he were in New York City talking about Central Park. Whatever else we might say about this word, we should acknowledge that when the crowds listening to Jesus heard him say "the Valley of Hinnom," their brains probably conjured up a very different mental picture than ours do when we hear the word "hell." Many or most of them had seen the place with their own two eyes.

Although Gehenna was a literal location, I'm not suggesting that Jesus was using the term in a literal way; he wasn't saying God would physically place people in this geographical location near Jerusalem. Rather, Gehenna is a metaphor for the consequences of our actions being returned on us in this life. Jesus was not actually the first person to use this metaphor this way! He borrowed it from the Hebrew prophet Jeremiah, who also used this image to describe the natural consequences of failing to live a life of love and connection with God, self, and others.

Why was such an ordinary real-life place so powerfully linked with evil and punishment? Because in the book of 2 Chronicles, in the Hebrew Bible, it is where the wicked king Ahaz burned his own children alive to sacrifice them to false gods. Some scholars have also speculated that the valley was used as a trash heap, where debris was consumed by fires that burned every hour of the day. It is unclear if it was a historical dump, but what we do know is that Gehenna came to be associated with fire, death, and the devastating ways that humanity brings harm on vulnerable people. Gehenna was a very specific metaphor for a very specific audience, who knew the dark spiritual and historical significance of that place.

So, yes, Jesus talks about Gehenna a lot, but if he's trying to describe the hell that so many modern Christians believe in, he's doing a very bad job. He does not describe it as a place of ongoing torment but as a place of death and destruction. For example, he says that God will "destroy [*not* torment] both soul and body in [Gehenna]" (Matthew 10:28). And while he does say it's a place "where their worm does not die and the fire is not quenched" (Mark 9:48, ESV), he's borrowing these images from Isaiah, where they refer to the consumption of dead bodies, not to people in torment. Jesus also compares being thrown into Gehenna to weeds being gathered and burned up completely (Matthew 13:40). Overall, the image of Gehenna is much more like the ruins of war than it is like an eternal torture chamber. Sure, if you have a certain set of preexisting biases, you can read hell into that, but there's no textual reason why you should.

Not only that, but the hell Jesus describes has nothing to do with "accepting Jesus into your heart" or becoming a Christian. Evangelicals (and most Protestants in general) believe that anyone who does not have "saving faith in Jesus Christ" is going to burn in hell, but Jesus never once connects Gehenna to what we believe. That seems like an odd oversight, considering the stakes. In the Bible, Jesus's warnings are not about right *believing*, but right *living*. Jesus warns religious leaders that their hypocritical actions are leading them to Gehenna; they're verbally abusing people and living in lust, while condemning these things in others.* Jesus says that Gehenna is for those who neglect the hungry, the thirsty, immigrants in need, the sick, and the imprisoned. It is not non-Christians, but those who show no concern for "the least of these" who are sent into the "punishment of the age."

By the way, that phrase comes from Matthew 25:46, and it's usually translated into English as "eternal punishment." We have been trained to read it as referring to never-ending torture, but that is not the obvious meaning. In the original Greek, the word we translate as "eternal" is *aionios*, which literally means "of the age." And the word for punishment is *kolasis*, which is used for corrective or restorative punishment

---

* Matthew 5:22 and Matthew 5:29–30, respectively.

(as opposed to the word for retributive punishment, *timoreo*). This has been acknowledged as far back as Clement of Alexandria (c. 150–215 CE), who translated the phrase as something more like "chastisement of the age."

But there's a larger point beyond the accuracy of the translation. Jesus said those who mistreat the oppressed will be punished. If we hear this and immediately start asking questions about how long the punishment will be, what kind of punishment it is, and who is going to be punished, then we are not hearing Jesus's true warning, which is, *If God is on the side of the oppressed, then we must be on the side of the oppressed.* When Jesus talked about Gehenna, he was not damning individual sinners to burn in hell for not "getting saved," he was showing us how to live and love in this world, and warning us of the suffering that our hypocrisy allows to go unchecked. Jesus did not teach a list of beliefs that people needed to agree with in order to stay out of hell; Jesus taught a spirituality of love, summed up by what we called *the golden rule.* In fact, the famous golden rule teaching also sums up Jesus's message of Gehenna:

> So whatever you wish that others would do to you, do also to them, for this is the Law and the Prophets. Enter by the narrow gate. For the gate is wide and the way is easy that leads to destruction, and those who enter by it are many. For the gate is narrow and the way is hard that leads to life, and those who find it are few.
>
> Matthew 7:12–14, ESV

The "narrow gate" is a favorite metaphor for hellfire preachers, who believe that they have the only way into heaven and that every other belief system will lead to hell. Many believe the "narrow gate" means that *the majority* of people who have ever lived are going to hell! But this passage makes it clear that the narrow way that leads to life is not a dogmatic belief; it is the way of love that Jesus taught: love for God, our neighbors, and ourselves. It's true that precious few people find this narrow gate. Compassionate, empathetic love—love that considers what life is like in someone else's shoes and comes from a place of solidarity—Jesus says that this is the summation of the Law and the Prophets. In other words, *living this way is what the whole Bible is about.*

So many Christians, especially evangelicals, tend to make the Bible about the afterlife, which causes them to interpret everything Jesus said to be about heaven or hell. But really, the Bible is about *this* life. The narrow gate isn't about going to heaven, and the wide gate isn't about going to hell. *It's about treating people in this world the way we would want to be treated.* We want health care for ourselves and our loved ones, so we should want everyone to have health care. We wouldn't want bombs dropping on our babies, so we should demand that our country stop dropping bombs on other people's babies. This difficult practice of solidarity and love—love for oneself, one's neighbors, and even one's enemies—leads to *life*: the wholeness and flourishing of the beloved community.

This is a narrow way; few there are that find it. It is easier to look out for "me and mine." Self-preservation and tribalism come naturally to us. Empathy is harder. The wide gate— the way of empires, the way of power, the way of "othering" and oppression—leads to a languishing downward spiral of violence and dehumanization. Jesus isn't talking about hell; he's talking about a world without love, without empathy and solidarity. Hell on earth. That is the meaning of Gehenna.

Apart from his warnings about Gehenna, Jesus only describes something resembling hell in the parable of the rich man and Lazarus. In this story, a beggar named Lazarus lives a life of poverty and suffering outside the gates of an un-named rich man who never helps him. When they die, Jesus depicts the rich man in torment in the flames of Hades. (Remember, Hades is translated from Sheol, and means the abode of the dead, and is not depicted as a place of torment anywhere else in the Bible.) Lazarus, on the other hand, is "carried . . . to Abraham's side" (Luke 16:22), which is a sort of shorthand for heaven. The rich man calls up to Abraham, begging him to send Lazarus to drip cool water on his tongue and provide some relief from the flames, but Abraham refuses.

As with the apocalyptic hyperbole in the book of Revelation, the fantastical details in this story remind us that we are listening to a metaphor, not a literal depiction of heaven or hell. Many preachers have tried to insist that this story is not a parable but rather actually depicts real people and real eternal consequences; very few modern scholars would agree. Even the most literal-minded evangelicals don't believe people in hell are having conversations with people in heaven, and using Abraham as a character is the first-century Jewish equivalent of invoking the image of St. Peter at the pearly gates. When someone in our day starts a story with that image, we know it's a common trope to evoke the idea of heaven. The point of the story is not that we should expect to stand in front of real gates made of real pearls when we die; more than likely, the point will be either the punchline of a joke or an ethical lesson. In Jesus's case, the point of his story is not that some people will be tortured by real flames while others will get to spend time with the real Abraham; the point is the urgency of justice and the danger of neglecting the poor.

Evangelicals who want to make this parable a literal account of the afterlife are in trouble, because salvation and judgment in this story look nothing like the gospel according to evangelicalism! In this story, heaven and hell have nothing to do with being "saved," "accepting Jesus into your heart," or "putting your faith in the work of the cross." Jesus is warning against mistreating the poor.

Some universalists interpret this story as a metaphor for how the wicked will be refined before they enter paradise. In other words, the torment the rich man experiences could be a picture of *restorative justice,* not just punishment. The story doesn't say the rich man will be tormented *forever*—perhaps he is being purged of his pride, being made fit for an eternity with God. However, I would join the majority of interpreters who caution against drawing any sort of definitive account of the afterlife from a parable. Jesus's parables use figurative language to communicate spiritual truths. This story is about how Jesus wants us to live, not about what happens when we die. Instead of trying to figure out the details of eternity from this story, we should simply receive its ethical lesson: God is on the side of the poor and forgotten, and we ignore them at our peril.

A REAL-WORLD WARNING

When we don't read the Bible in its historical context, we may miss things that would have been very obvious to the original readers. What many people miss when they read Jesus's warnings is that Jesus of Nazareth was a Jewish prophet in a long line of Jewish prophets. The prophets that we know from the Hebrew Bible, or Old Testament, use apocalyptic language, and to modern-day readers, they can sound like they're talking about the last judgment and the end of the world. But they're actually just talking about the end of *their* world: the destruction of the Northern Kingdom of Israel by the Assyrians in 722 BCE or the destruction of the Temple and Jerusalem by the Babylonians in 597 BCE.

Like the prophets before him, Jesus appeared prior to a major catastrophe and warned of coming destruction. He preached an urgent message, because he was born into a society on the brink of collapse. And indeed, in 70 CE, about forty years after his crucifixion, Jerusalem would be razed to the ground by Roman armies and the Temple left a heap of rubble, for the second time in history. There really *was* weeping and gnashing of teeth—not in the afterlife, but in Jerusalem.

History was repeating itself. Six hundred years earlier, Jeremiah prophesied that Jerusalem and its Temple would be destroyed by the Babylonians, as God's punishment for the kingdom of Judah's religious hypocrisy, violence, exclusion, and neglect of the poor. When Jeremiah warned that their nation and Temple would be destroyed, he said "the Valley of Ben Hinnom"—that's the Hebrew name for Gehenna—would become known as the "Valley of Slaughter" because it would be completely full of dead bodies (Jeremiah 7:32). (Jeremiah, as you can see, was very metal.)

But as extreme as this language sounds, the Valley of Slaughter was not a fiery hell in the afterlife. Jeremiah was speaking of the very real, very historical slaughter that was on its way in the form of Babylonian chariots, swords, and spears. Jeremiah was not warning Jerusalem that God would punish them in the afterlife but that the consequences of their actions would return on them in this life.

Jesus used the apocalyptic metaphor of Gehenna in the same way Jeremiah did: to warn a corrupt establishment that if things didn't radically change, they would find themselves in the rubble of their own dirty rotten system, a system that privileged the powerful, while excluding the poor and vulnerable. As biblical scholar Nik Ansell puts it, "all of Jesus's references to Gehenna, which are widely thought by believer and nonbeliever alike to refer to a last judgment at the end of time, are actually about the coming judgment on Israel, Jerusalem, and its temple."

In his most vehement condemnation of the corrupt religious and political elites, Jesus clearly connects the warning of Gehenna to the approaching fall of Jerusalem:

> *Woe to you, scribes and Pharisees, hypocrites! . . . You serpents, you brood of vipers, how are you to escape being sentenced to hell [Gehenna]? . . . Truly, I say to you, all these things will come upon* <u>this generation</u>. *. . . See, your house is left to you desolate.*
>
> Matthew 23:29–38, ESV, emphasis mine

When Jesus declares that the religious elite will not escape the fires of Gehenna, he is not speaking of a postmortem judgment inflicted by a God who demands satisfaction for sin. He is lamenting over Jerusalem, over the desolation that is coming to "this generation" in particular, because they cared more about religious purity laws than about "the weightier matters of the law: justice and mercy" (Matthew 23:23, ESV).

By the time the Gospel of Matthew was written, Jesus's warnings about Jerusalem had already come to pass. In fact, the contemporary Jewish historian Josephus tells us that when Rome destroyed Jerusalem, bodies were thrown over the city walls into the valley of Gehenna because there was no space to bury them. The author of Matthew would have known this; he may have even *seen* it. Matthew was written for a Jewish audience who had recently survived this atrocity and were struggling to make sense of how God could have allowed Jerusalem to be destroyed—again. The Temple, the symbol of God's presence, lay in ruins for the second time in history, and everyone was reeling from the loss of their homes, their country, their place of worship, their community, their imagined future. The dream of a free Jerusalem was buried in the rubble along with their dead. To imagine that Matthew's Jesus was discussing some abstract notion of postmortem punishment, disconnected from this life-defining catastrophe, is to entirely miss the point. It trivializes their suffering and the urgency of Jesus's real-world message.

We have been trained to think that the point of the Bible is to tell us how to achieve the afterlife we want. We easily forget that the people in the biblical world had the same concerns that we do. In the ways that matter most, their world was just like our world, and their concerns were the same as our concerns. They were plagued by poverty and food scarcity, worried about impending war, and burdened by corrupt political rulers—the same kinds of things that keep us up at night today. Their concerns are the flesh-and-blood matters of real life. That's what biblical authors were thinking about as they were writing, and it's what their original audiences were thinking about when they read or heard these texts. This is good news, because it means that Jesus's message is relevant for our world, not just the world to come. Jesus did not preach a bloodless message, disconnected from the needs of bodily life.

Many of us were raised with a trite, disembodied Christianity that neglects the conditions of the disinherited people of this earth and focuses on the rewards of heaven or the punishments of hell. But this is not the message of the Bible! The Bible is a book with dirt under its fingernails. It digs into the material reality of the world we live in. Theologian Harold Wells explains that the history of the Bible

> has to do with social and economic relationships. It has to do with finding new land (Abraham), with emancipation from slavery (Moses), with international war

and struggles for hegemony (Jeremiah), with class struggles between the rich and powerful, and the poor and the weak (Amos). . . . Nothing could be more earthy or "material" than the story of the relationship between the Spirit of Yahweh and the people of Israel. Nothing could be more fleshly than the story of the incarnation of God in the human Jesus, his eating and drinking with marginalized folk, his engagement in the social struggles of his time and place, his bloody execution by crucifixion, and his bodily resurrection to life. The biblical story of God's engagement with human history is a story of flesh and blood, of history and political struggle.

Karl Marx famously called religion "the opiate of the masses." In Marx's view, most religious belief is used to numb the people at the bottom of the socioeconomic hierarchy to the nature of their condition, so that the rich and powerful can continue to get away with their injustices. If our Christianity ignores material conditions in a world of extreme inequality, fails to preach justice during apartheid and segregation, and does not make peace when genocides are underway, all because the only thing we care about is hell, then Marx was unquestionably right. When we reduce salvation and judgment to issues of the next life, we abandon this life and this earth to those who would exploit it.

Jesus did not do this. Jesus did not come to anesthetize people with abstract promises. He came to awaken them to the reality of their situation. Jesus, like Jeremiah, warned that if people continued in a state of disconnection, despising instead of loving their neighbor, then the natural consequences of sin—Gehenna—would fall on their heads. Their oppressive, exclusionary tendencies would lead to their destruction.

This message was political—the kind of message that could get you killed. The kind of message that could save the world.

CHICKENS COMING HOME TO ROOST

Hell is the natural consequence of our actions, not punishment from God. God does not punish sin in the way we punish each other. *Sin is its own punishment.* Richard Rohr says that "we are punished not *for* our sins, but *by* our sins." When the Bible talks about God's "wrath," it's not some cosmic temper tantrum. God does not get dysregulated and punch a wall like a jilted ex-lover when we sin. Anger and wrath are anthropomorphic metaphors for speaking of the natural consequences of our sin that happen when people or nations don't live in line with God's love.

Maybe you've heard that sin means "missing the mark." This doesn't just mean "doing the wrong thing." *It means missing the whole point of life.* "The wages of sin is death" (Romans 6:23), because life is about love and connection, and sin is what disconnects us from God, ourselves, and each other. Sin is forgetting that we are all a part of this together. The alienation and estrangement of sin is its own punishment—it always leads to death.

A modern-day prophet who pointed out how our national sins would return on us is Rev. Dr. Jeremiah Wright Jr., pastor emeritus of Trinity United Church of Christ in Chicago. When I consider how the powers of Jesus's day reacted to his warnings about Gehenna, I find myself thinking of the political crucifixion of Dr. Wright. During the 2008 US presidential campaign, then-senator Barack Obama came under fire in the media for attending Wright's church. The focus of the controversy was a sermon Wright preached immediately following the terrorist attacks of September 11, in which he lamented America's sins and global acts of violence.

As someone raised with very conservative politics and a belief in America's inherent goodness, I was quite shocked by clips of the sermon at the time, but in retrospect, I agree with every word. Wright tells an alternative history, a history from the margins, a history told by the victims instead of the superpower. He enumerates the atrocities the US has perpetrated against the world, from slavery and the genocide of Native Americans, to dropping nuclear bombs on Japan, to bombing civilians in Grenada, Panama, and Sudan. "And now," he concludes, "we are indignant because the stuff we have done overseas is now brought right back to our own front yards. America's chickens are coming home to roost! Violence begets violence. Hatred begets hatred. And terrorism begets terrorism."

Of course, the terrorist attacks of 9/11 were evil. The global violence of the American military industrial complex does not justify the violence that terrorists returned upon America. Wright is simply pointing out that this is how violence works. We reap what we sow. *When you sow violence, you reap Gehenna.*

Under political pressure, Obama distanced himself from Wright. But Wright's core message, like Jesus's, still rings true. The global violence America perpetrates comes back around, even as we claim innocence. Instead of learning the lesson of this powerful sermon, the American response to 9/11 was to start not one but two wars of greed and revenge. The cycle of violence continued to the tune of more than 300,000 Iraqi civilian deaths and more than 70,000 Afghan civilian deaths. And the American Empire, the wealthiest nation in the history of the world, still spends trillions on bombs while saying that it can't afford to provide health care, child-care, or housing to its people. Until we beat our swords into plowshares, this violence will come home to roost again and again and again.

Like Wright's message, Jesus's warnings about Gehenna also struck a nerve. Is it any wonder he was executed by the state? Nobody gets crucified for talking about the afterlife. Jesus was killed because his message threatened the powers that be in *this* life.

The message of Gehenna is not about a distant, disconnected hell waiting for us after death if we fail to say the right prayer, and it isn't just a message for past centuries. It is repeated throughout history, into our present moment. In the first century, hell was on earth in the ruins of Jerusalem. In 2024, hell was on earth in Gaza. Hell is always on earth. The message of Gehenna is about the very real hells we create, and suffer in, right now, when we fail to live out God's love and justice in the world. It's about the hell of systemic racism and mass incarceration. The hell of endless wars and refugee crises. The hell of wealth hoarding amid desperate poverty. The hell of a planet dying while corporate powers block action on climate change.

How do we build a world where Gehenna—hell on earth— is not our lived reality? What does it look like to turn from the sins that breed poverty, violence, and oppression? These are the issues Jesus spoke to, and died for. His warnings, though stark, came from a place of love and longing: "Jerusalem, Jerusalem, . . . how often I have longed to gather your children together, as a hen gathers her chicks under her wings, and you were not willing" (Matthew 23:37). As a prophet, Jesus did not just want to *reveal* a bleak future for Jerusalem—he wanted to *change* their future! His whole mission was a call to change.

But the message of Gehenna is not just a message of

suffering; it is a message of justice and hope for the victims of history. It says that the systems of empire and domination, which loom so large in this world, will not have the final word. Their violence will ultimately return on them. God's justice will prevail. A new world awaits on the other side of the hells we create. Jesus's warning is a call to action, a call to care about what God cares about.

So let us not spiritualize Jesus's words into vague threats of a fiery afterlife. Let us hear them as the urgent wake-up call they are: to see the hells around us, and within us, and commit to the hard work of repentance and repair; to build a world where "the least of these" can flourish and where God's love and justice are known on earth, as they are in heaven. The alternative is hell.

But hell is never the end of the story.

7.

ALL IN ALL

*If There's No Hell,
What About Heaven?*

I take literally the statement in the Gospel of John that God loves the world. . . . I believe that divine love . . . summons the world always toward wholeness, which ultimately is reconciliation . . . with God.

—Wendell Berry

Since I talk all the time about how I don't believe in hell, I am often asked if I believe in heaven. Fair question. The short answer is yes, but I don't really know what it means. Every picture we have in the Bible that describes heaven is metaphorical and ambiguous. When we speak of streets of gold, God wiping away our tears, a new Jerusalem, and a river of life, we are using metaphors for spiritual realities that are beyond the limits of language. We are naming what cannot be named.

Universalism is the belief that every single person will ultimately be reconciled to God. I call myself a universalist, because I believe that God's love is universal and that in the end "all shall be well, and all manner of thing shall be well," as the medieval Christian mystic Julian of Norwich said. There are many kinds of Christian universalists. Some believe in purgatory, where wicked people will experience a finite period of correction that purges them of evil, making them fit for heaven. Others simply believe everyone goes to heaven, whatever that may mean. I personally do not know. I am happily agnostic about the specifics.

What I do know is that whatever it looks like, the story of this big, beautiful universe God made has a happy ending. I believe that, not just because it is emotionally satisfying to me or because it fits with the character of God but also because the Bible tells me so. In the last chapter, we looked at what the Bible really says about hell and why so much of what we've been taught about hell makes no sense when you look at it without the bias of modern conservative theology. In this chapter, we'll look at how, despite what we may have heard, it makes perfect sense to read the Bible's message as one of universal reconciliation.

THE BIBLICAL CASE FOR UNIVERSALISM

As I've said, you can find evidence for just about anything you want in the Bible. But the biblical case for hell pales in comparison to the much stronger biblical evidence that God is going to restore *all creation* and draw every single creature back into all-encompassing love. I may not know what that is going to look like, but I'm here for it.

In fact, people committed to the doctrine of hell are forced to ignore and minimize these promises of ultimate restoration, even though they show up with more clarity and more frequency than verses about hell.

I don't believe that stacking up "proof texts" is the best way to argue for any position, whether hell or universal salvation. But I do think it's ironic that hellfire Christians often act like the Bible is on their side and that universalists "get squishy" with the biblical text in order to see what they want to see, when in reality, the opposite is true. If evangelicals are going to be biblical literalists, they should probably understand that the word *all* literally means "all" in such verses as these (emphases mine):

> For as in Adam all die, so in Christ <u>all</u> will be made alive.
>
> 1 Corinthians 15:22

> And I, when I am lifted up from the earth, will draw <u>all</u> people to myself.
>
> John 12:32

Just as one trespass resulted in condemnation for <u>all</u> people, so also one righteous act resulted in justification and life for <u>all</u> people.

Romans 5:18

For God has bound everyone over to disobedience so that he may have mercy on them <u>all</u>.

Romans 11:32

If conservatives believe *fire* literally means "fire," then logically, they should also believe that *the world* literally means "the world" in such verses as these:

I did not come to judge the world, but to save <u>the world</u>.

John 12:47

We know that this is indeed the Savior of <u>the world</u>.

John 4:42, ESV

And we have seen and testify that the Father has sent his Son to be the Savior of <u>the world</u>.

1 John 4:14

And he is the atonement for our sins, and not for ours only but also for the sins of <u>the whole world</u>.

1 John 2:2*

Many Christians presume that God's will is to punish people for eternity, based on several unclear passages. I wish those same Christians would also learn about God's ultimate

---

* This is based on David Bentley Hart's translation of the verse in *The New Testament* (New Haven: Yale University Press, 2023), 480.

hope for creation from the passages that speak clearly of all things being fully restored and redeemed:

> *He has made known to us the mystery of his will, according to his good pleasure that he set forth in Christ, as a plan for the fullness of time, to gather up all things in him, things in heaven and things on earth.*
>
> Ephesians 1:9–10, NRSV

> *For in him all the fullness of God was pleased to dwell, and through him God was pleased to reconcile to himself all things, whether on earth or in heaven, by making peace through the blood of his cross.*
>
> Colossians 1:19–20, NRSV

> *For he must reign until he has put all his enemies under his feet. The last enemy to be destroyed is death. . . . When he has done this, then the Son himself will be made subject to him who put everything under him, so that God may be all in all.*
>
> 1 Corinthians 15:25–26, 28

If hell is the end of the story for the majority of people who have ever lived, I do not know how we could rightly say that God is "all in all." If countless people will continue to consciously exist in a state of suffering and separation from God, then it is not true that God will ultimately "reconcile to himself all things." If only Christians are reconciled to God, that isn't all things. It's not even *most* things! At best, it's some things. *The story is better than that.*

But this story of ultimate reconciliation is not just a stack of Bible verses. It is a key theme of the whole Bible, and it is essential to how we relate to God. We connect to God and love God because God first loves us. God is not a punisher; God is a healer. We fail, but God's steadfast love "endures forever"—Psalm 136 repeats this truth twenty-six times! The redundant message doesn't make for the most subtle poetry, but some truths need to be drilled into thick skulls. Despite the way that Christian history shows how we are experts at missing the point, those who know God best have always known that at the very heart of God is unfailing love.

When I was a pastor, the church members whose faith excited me the most were often in the recovery community. We hosted AA in our church building weekly and helped start a sober living home in our small town. Without fail, it was always these Christians, with what some might call a "checkered past," who best understood the grace of God. They knew that there was a higher power who was not giving up on them and never would. They believed that God really would restore all things, because they had experienced restoration firsthand.

My friend Eric, a former heroin addict, couldn't shut up about how Jesus saved his life. Eric was on the verge of suicide when he met Jesus, and his life was turned around. Since then, he's gotten married, had a kid, and held down a decent job. He would proudly declare that he was a total fuckup, and that if Jesus could have grace for him, Jesus had grace for anyone and everyone. When Eric said it, I really believed it.

Many church people go through the motions of worship but lack a deeply felt awareness of God's expansive love. Their knowledge of God's love is often theoretical until their lives are marked by the desperation that comes from suffering or failure. My friends in recovery know firsthand what reconciliation means. Many of them have had to make amends with friends and family, some of them multiple times. Some of them have permanently lost connections with loved ones, even their children. And yet they know that no matter what happens in life, God is not giving up on them. God *could* not; it would be opposed to God's essential character. God is in the restoration business. This is grace. This is gospel. And this awareness of God's character does not make sense at all if hell is a part of the story.

A God who is unrelentingly forgiving in life cannot become a merciless tyrant in death. A story about a God whose steadfast love endures forever cannot end with most of God's precious creatures suffering in hell. A God who is "compassionate and gracious, slow to anger, abounding in love" (Psalm 103:8) and who "does not treat us as our sins deserve or repay us according to our iniquities" (Psalm 103:10) will not, upon our death, suddenly unload an eternity of torment on us for those same iniquities. Hell would create a self-contradictory picture of God. Thankfully, that is not the God revealed in the Bible, and that is not the story the Bible is telling.

Unlike the doctrine of hell, which is never clearly spelled out in the Bible, the unrelenting, restorative love of God—which does not count our sins against us but instead works all things together for good in order not only to redeem people from every tribe, tongue, and nation but also to liberate all of creation—is spelled out in the Bible time and time again.* It is arguably the unifying theme of the whole book. Over and over, the people of the Bible are drawn into the unrelenting love of God on the other side of their failures.

FROM JUDGMENT TO RESTORATION

Although God is often depicted as a judge, the trajectory of scripture is unignorable: The story always moves from judg-

---

* See 2 Corinthians 5:19, Romans 8:28, and Romans 8:21, respectively.

ment to restoration. This is so pervasive in scripture that it is impossible to miss. This is how God relates not only to the people of Israel but also even to the nations that do not acknowledge Israel's God. Over and over, judgment is pronounced, and then, surprise! (No surprise at all!) God restores.

Here is just one example among hundreds. In this passage, Jeremiah (you know, the guy who talked about Gehenna before Jesus did) is pronouncing God's judgment on his nation for their sins. God says that this time, the judgment will be *irreversible.*

> *This is what the LORD says:*
> *Your wound is incurable,*
> *your injury beyond healing . . .*
> *because your guilt is so great*
> *and your sins so many.*
>
> Jeremiah 30:12, 14

This pronouncement of judgment sounds severe. There are no second chances. The wound is incurable, beyond healing; there is no remedy. *The Bible is clear.* There is no coming back from this.

And yet, just a breath later:

> *"But I will restore you to health*
> *and heal your wounds,"*
> *declares the LORD.*
>
> Jeremiah 30:17

If you think that looks like a contradiction, *you're right.* "Your wound is incurable" is about as definitive and clearcut as it gets. And yet, God goes on to promise to restore the nation to health and heal their wounds. Because God doesn't mind contradicting God's own word for the sake of healing her beloved.

Over and over, the violence and sin of humanity lead to calamity, but God's loving-kindness perseveres past any breaking point. With God's love, it turns out, there is no breaking point. Instead, there is a pattern of natural consequences followed by restored wholeness. The story with God never ends until it moves into restoration, even for the most cursed places. One of the most powerful examples of this is the city of Sodom, one of the most despised cities in scripture. Sodom is used again and again as an illustration of how and why God judges people and nations.

Despite conservative rhetoric you may have heard, God does not judge Sodom for being "gay" but because its inhabitants "were arrogant, overfed and unconcerned; they did not help the poor and needy" (Ezekiel 16:49). And just like it always does, the violence and oppression of Sodom came home to roost. Every empire that chooses violence over love will reap what it sows. Sodom is the prototypical example of what happens when cities and communities turn their back on the poor—so it is quite shocking that the Bible promises restoration, even for Sodom!

> *I will restore their fortunes, the fortunes of Sodom and her daughters and the fortunes of Samaria and her daughters, and I will restore your own fortunes along with theirs.*
>
> Ezekiel 16:53, NRSV

The story is never over until God brings restoration. If this is true for Sodom, it's true for every condemned person and every cursed place. Even Gehenna.

In the last chapter, we saw how Jesus used the image of Gehenna, the Valley of Slaughter, to talk about the fate of people who refuse to live in God's love. Although there is disagreement as to whether Jesus used the term *Gehenna* to refer to this life or the next life, it is clear that it was a place of judgment. A place for "sinners." And by all accounts, it sounded like the end of the line. The worm does not die, and the fire is not quenched. The judgment is final, irreversible.

But no. Even in the Valley of Slaughter, the story isn't over until love wins:

> *The whole valley of the dead bodies and the ashes . . .*
> *shall be sacred to the LORD. It shall not be plucked up*
> *or overthrown anymore forever.*
>
> Jeremiah 31:40, NRSV

Jeremiah says a day is coming when even the Valley of Slaughter will be a sacred place. Like the Christmas hymn says, God's blessings will be known "far as the curse is found." *Every curse is undone in the end.*

Weeping and gnashing of teeth are a part of life. They are often the result of our decisions. We have all acted cruelly, and have had cruelty visited upon us. We have wept, and we have been the cause of weeping. Sometimes, especially when we are in the middle of it, we feel that our story will end there. In our worst moments, we can even feel that this would be the end that we deserve. But this is never God's end for her beloved.

> *For [God's] anger lasts only a moment,*
> *but [God's] favor lasts a lifetime!*

Weeping may stay for the night,
but rejoicing comes in the morning.

Psalm 30:5

God's "anger" is never ultimate. It is only ever *penultimate*. Even for the worst sinners. It can't be any different. This seems to be built into creation, built into the nature of God.

THE NATURE OF GOD

What is God like? Well, the Bible is a *multivocal* book, meaning that it speaks through multiple voices and perspectives, which may sometimes be contradictory. (It is not, despite what conservative Christians may tell you, *univocal*, speaking from a single, perfectly consistent perspective.) This ancient, complex book paints various pictures of God, some of which are quite violent. As a result, many of us don't know on a day-to-day basis what kind of God we're going to wake up to. Am I going to be greeted by the God who commanded the Israelites to slay every man, woman, and child in Canaan today? Or the God who compares herself to a nursing mother, who could never possibly forget her children?

For many of us, even though we were told that God is love and tried our best to believe it, it didn't seem like love had the final word. Hell had the final word. But that story does not make any sense, especially not if God is revealed to us in Jesus Christ.

Now, if you're reading this book, you may not be a Christian anymore. (You may never have been one.) Maybe you don't believe God is revealed to us in Jesus—maybe you don't believe in God at all. But I think it's important to look at what Christianity says about who God is, because if any Christians have ever told you that God will send you to hell, it's important for you to know that, no matter what you believe now, those Christians got it wrong.

Why did they get it wrong? Because Christians believe that Jesus reveals the character of God; he pulls back the curtain on what God has always been like. And Jesus never punishes anyone. Not a single time. Jesus only heals. Because God is not a punisher, but a healer.

We see this clearly when Jesus says, "The Father judges *no one,* but has entrusted all judgment to the Son" (John 5:22, emphasis mine). The way that God judges is revealed to us in the way that Jesus judges. And to confirm what his followers already knew to be true just by walking with him, just by being in his compassionate presence, Jesus makes it plain: "You judge by human standards. I pass judgment on *no one*" (John 8:15, emphasis mine).

The Father does not judge but entrusts judgment to Jesus. And Jesus does not judge like we judge. We're the ones who punish. We judge by human standards of retribution. Only in the last few decades have people begun to formally study how *restorative justice* methods compare to those of *retributive justice,* and the data from these experiments in our penal systems confirm what Jesus has said all along: Retribution doesn't work. Retributive justice is no justice at all. It is revenge.

We see this trajectory away from punishment toward restoration in the way the Bible talks about God. In Hosea 11, God explicitly expresses their own growth away from judgment toward mercy. God laments,

> *How can I give you up, O Ephraim?*
> *How can I hand you over, O Israel? . . .*

> *My heart recoils within me;*
> *my compassion grows warm and tender.*

I will not execute my burning anger;
  I will not again destroy Ephraim;
for I am God and not a man.

Hosea 11:8–9, ESV

The Hebrew Bible scholar Walter Brueggemann says that this passage tells "the whole story of God's life as a recovering practitioner of violence." According to Brueggemann, when God says, "I am God and not a man," God is telling us, "You've got me all wrong. I'm not like you. I'm not some big violent guy."

Now, we have to be honest about the fact that very often in the Bible, God does seem to act like a big violent guy. No matter how much we try, many of us have a very difficult time breaking the mental picture of God as a big violent guy, far away from us, probably on a throne. But passages like this explicitly move us away from that picture. We are meant to follow this spiritual trajectory. Richard Rohr points out that "God grows more and more *nonviolent* through the Scriptures . . . this evolution becomes completely obvious in Jesus." Of course this doesn't mean that God changes. It is our *awareness* of God that changes.

This evolution of our understanding of God is always moving from judgment toward mercy, from exclusion toward reconciliation. In many ancient scriptures, God seems to be a tribal God. Yahweh, the God of Israel, is pitted against the gods of other nations: our god versus theirs. But that is not the final picture of God. This view is repudiated by the prophets of the Hebrew Bible, and the coming of Jesus pushes the narrative even further toward universalism.* In 1 John,

---

* In the prophets, see for example Isaiah 2:2–4; 25:6–8; 55:1–11; 56:6–8; 60:11–14; and Zechariah 8:20–23.

one of the latest written books of the Bible, we finally get the majestic definition that "God is love." There is nothing more universal than love; it is the inheritance of all people, and it's where the story is heading.

For everybody.

A QUESTION OF JUSTICE

At this point you might be asking: Reconciliation for *everybody*? Really? What about Hitler? What about the evildoers who escape justice in this lifetime? What about the oppressors who cause untold suffering and seem to get away with it? Do they also deserve ultimate restoration?

One of the primary arguments against universal reconciliation is that it can feel like letting perpetrators off the hook too easily. I think we should acknowledge that even the worst human being imaginable does not deserve a *never-ending* punishment for crimes committed in one finite human life, but I do understand the need for justice. Some people create hell for others in this life and get away with it. This is a serious problem, especially for younger generations, who are more aware than ever before of the great injustices happening all over the world.

There is much to celebrate in recent movements calling for justice. For example, the #MeToo movement declared that enough is enough; there can be no more impunity for abusive men to go on abusing. The Black Lives Matter movement has similarly taken a stand against police brutality. Empty apologies won't cut it—there must be a reckoning.

If we believe in universalism for everyone, even the worst perpetrators, does that mean we don't care about justice? Quite simply, no. The story of the Bible teaches that justice is not incompatible with restoration—in fact, the greatest and most powerful examples of justice are always working toward ultimate restoration.

Martin Luther King Jr. exemplified this notion, and he often spoke of how white supremacists were also in bondage— they needed to be liberated from hate. True justice works for the liberation of the oppressed as well as the oppressor, and recognizes that because we are all in this together, none are free until all are free, oppressors included.

One of the most powerful examples I've ever heard of mercy and justice weaving together with the goal of restoration is the Truth and Reconciliation Commission (TRC) in South Africa after the abolition of apartheid. Apartheid was a system of racial segregation based on white supremacy that was the law of the land in South Africa until 1994. When it finally fell, there was deep, painful division in the country after generations of race-based oppression and marginalization.

Anglican Bishop Desmond Tutu initiated the TRC to address the hurt. The TRC set up public hearings where victims could share their stories of the horrific crimes they endured under apartheid. Recognizing that restoration was more important than punishing every crime, Tutu established a system of amnesty: Perpetrators who came forward and fully confessed their crimes in televised hearings would be pardoned. The condition was full disclosure; total amnesty only came with total acknowledgment of the atrocities committed. The crimes were horrific, and there were too many to count, much less prosecute. Stories were told of sons dragged away in the night by security police, stories of daughters sexually assaulted by white men.

Despite criticism from those who felt the TRC was a miscarriage of justice or that dwelling on past crimes would hinder healing, Tutu's plan proved to be a balm for the country. The public hearings acknowledged the victims' pain, and even though the perpetrators were pardoned, they had to admit the grievousness of their actions. Tutu believed in forgiveness, but he knew it was demanding. He said, "Forgiveness is not cheap. It is costly. Reconciliation is not easy. It cost God the death of his only begotten Son." The TRC demonstrated that true justice involves truth-telling, repentance, and repair—not merely punishment. It was truth and reconciliation, not punishment, that allowed the country to move forward.

Believing that God will restore all things and all people does not mean ignoring or minimizing the reality of evil and oppression in this world. Reconciliation is no bloodless thing. God does not dismiss oppressors; on the cross, God exposes them. God enters into the struggle of human injustice and takes the side of the victims of oppression, even unto death. I don't know how God will be perfectly just and also reconcile all things, but I don't know how God does a lot of things. We get a possible hint in a mysterious and ambiguous verse (as almost all verses about final judgment are) in which the apostle Paul talks about a day when everything will be exposed, "for the day will disclose it, because it will be revealed by fire" (1 Corinthians 3:13, ESV). This is not a fire of torment but a fire that exposes and burns away what is false. All our ego, our pretenses, and our false selves—everything that is not rooted in love will be tested by fire. Paul concludes, "If anyone's work is burned up, he will suffer loss, though he himself will be saved, but only as through fire" (1 Corinthians 3:15, ESV). Even this person whose work is tested and shown to be wanting *is saved*.

Some people have cocooned themselves in layers of falsehood. They are so deeply stuck in the lies they believe about themselves, God, and other people that there is hardly anything left of their true self, to the extent that when it's all burned up, there is hardly a person left. The image of God in them is barely a flickering spark. But even that person can be saved, as through fire. The stamp of divinity is still there, underneath it all, and the true self will return to love, along with everything else in all creation.

We can affirm the need for justice and work for accountability and restitution for wrongs done, even as we hold to the hope that none of God's beloved creatures are beyond the reach of redemption. Endless punishment is not required for God to be just, and as important as justice is, we are not meant to be fixated on it at the expense of love. As the poet and environmental activist Wendell Berry has said, "The Christian gospel is a summons to peace, calling for justice beyond anger, mercy beyond justice, forgiveness beyond mercy, love beyond forgiveness." God's justice results in restoration for all, because the truest form of justice leads to love. Victim and perpetrator alike will be made whole.

THE INVITATION IS ALWAYS OPEN

In the closing scenes of the Bible, in the book of Revelation, we see a vision that many Christians believe depicts the last things: heaven and hell. As I've said, I don't believe we're meant to read this apocalyptic vision literally, but we can see a powerful picture of hope and universal salvation in it.

First, at the end of Revelation 20, John, the author of the text, sees a lake of fire. Death and Hades are thrown in, as a metaphorical symbol that death itself is defeated. Then, anyone whose name is not found in the book of life is thrown into the fiery lake. John says, "This is the second death, the lake of fire" (Revelation 20:14, NRSV). This seems incredibly final.

But the visual journey continues into Revelation 21 and

22, where John sees a vision of the new heaven and new earth. This city is the fulfillment of all the hopes of the prophets: "Nation shall not lift up sword against nation; neither shall they learn war any more" (Isaiah 2:4, NRSV). This is a world experiencing the peace of God.

But then something very strange happens that doesn't fit the standard evangelical narrative at all. At this point, the so-called *unsaved* are supposed to be burning in the lake of fire while the "saved" peacefully enjoy their eternal bliss, right? But no: John sees the wicked standing right outside of the gates of the New Jerusalem (Revelation 22:14–15)! And we are told that those who enter the gates only have to wash their robes, and they too can experience the wholeness of God's kingdom. This is not an exclusive city, only for the "saved" or the people with the right religion. We don't have to wonder if the gates will open to these people, because Revelation 21:25 (NRSV) dramatically says of the city that "its gates will never be shut." This city has an open-door policy!

So the wicked are outside of the gates, *but the gates are wide open.* They just have to wash their robes, and they can come right in. This is a metaphor for repentance, for experiencing what some Christians may call *the new birth* or *salvation*. But in John's vision, it comes *after* the so-called *final judgment*! With a God of unrelenting love, can any judgment be "final"? Here is the powerful conclusion to this image, which is one of the last verses in the entire Bible:

> *The Spirit and the Bride say, "Come." And let the one who hears say, "Come." And let the one who is thirsty come; let the one who desires take the water of life without price.*
>
> Revelation 22:17, ESV

Who is this invitation for? Not for the "righteous." They're already in the city, already drinking from the river of life. This invitation is for the "wicked" who are outside of the city gates. They are told that they can join in on the party and enter into the peace of God. They can drink the water of life, without price. It was always free. It was always available to them. The invitation is always open.

Evangelicals have been told that the lake of fire is the ultimate fate, that this judgment is final and irreversible. Not only does that defy the repeated pattern of scripture, it also contradicts the very picture we are given at the close of the Bible in the book of Revelation! Even if we insist on taking these apocalyptic, metaphorical images literally, judgment does not have the last word. The welcoming love of God has the last word. The last word is "Come."

Now, the purpose of these symbolic images is not to give us a dogmatic picture of who's in, who's out, and what heaven and hell are going to look like. We should approach all of these pictures with humility and curiosity. But what I do know is that, even with all its frightening images, this book is still telling a good story about creation. A story that ends in hell for *anybody* would be a tragic story. The story of creation would not be good news if even one of God's beloved creatures was tormented for eternity. The story ends with creation being fully restored. With all creatures coming to drink together of the water of life in the new heaven and new earth. I have to be honest—I don't believe that this is a literal image at all. But I know at the very least it means we will drink deeply of the love of God. We will be reunited with the love that we came from.

I think it's poignant that the story ends with an *invitation* to restoration rather than spelling it out. The Spirit says, "Come!" This is always true for us. This invitation is alive for us. It comes to us, even now. We can step more deeply into the peace of God, right now. Just like the father in the parable of the prodigal son, pleading with his elder son to lay down his superiority complex and join the celebration, the Spirit never stops beckoning us to join in on the party God is throwing.

This book of Revelation is not ultimately telling us what's *going* to happen: who's going to burn, and when. This book is inviting us to come drink of the water of life, now. We can wash our robes of violence and oppression and take up the cause of the poor, right now. Participate in the healing of the nations, right now. And as we do, we can enter into the peace that God desires for all of creation. Everyone can get in on this.

In the first few chapters of this book, I explored how the traditional doctrine of hell creates disconnection in our spiritual lives. It disconnects us from ourselves, as we internalize the message that we are worthy of damnation. It disconnects us from others, as we divide humanity into the saved and the damned. And it disconnects us from God, as we struggle to trust in the unconditional love of a punitive deity. But although we can find punishment in the Bible if we are looking for it, the ultimate trajectory of reconciliation points us to a different story, which leads to a very different spirituality. The more we are drawn into the love of God—the God who is not a punisher but a healer—the more we are set free to love and accept ourselves, embrace others, and connect with God.

8.

GETTING CURIOUS

What We Don't Need the Bible to Tell Us

People without imagination really have no right to write about ultimate things.

—Reinhold Niebuhr

We've spent the last two chapters taking an in-depth look at the scriptural evidence for hell (which is weak) and the scriptural evidence for universal reconciliation (which is strong). But now I want to pause for a moment to reflect on the fact that scripture isn't everything. I know this idea can feel shocking for many Christians, especially evangelicals. We're used to looking to the Bible to support every last one of our ideas or opinions. But it's not a step-by-step instruction manual. Yes, if you're a Christian, you should pay attention to the Bible as a sacred text, but at some point we have to recognize that we simply *don't have all the answers* and *never will*. To that end, in this chapter, we'll approach the idea of deconstructing hell from a perspective based not on the Bible but on an open-minded and open-hearted spirituality by leaning into curiosity, uncertainty, and our own intuition. Many of us were taught that certainty was holy and doubt was dangerous. But what if curiosity itself could be sacred? What if our questions could lead us deeper into love rather than away from God?

A LOVE AFFAIR WITH CERTITUDE

One thing I don't miss about being an evangelical pastor is having to have the answer for everything. The need to be right, to have certainty on almost every issue, was a key feature of being a good Christian leader in evangelicalism. My friend Doug Hammack calls this the evangelical "love affair with certitude," and it is required by a spirituality of hell. If hell is real, then nothing is more important than being certain we aren't going there. Once I stopped believing in hell, I was able to start relaxing into being comfortable with uncertainty. If you're not going to burn forever for being wrong about doctrinal issues, you have the freedom to be curious. To explore. To ask, What beliefs serve me? What beliefs lead me deeper into love? What spiritual ideas open me up to be the kind of person I want to be, the best and most loving version of myself? These questions are frightening to someone finding their safety in certitude, but I believe they are spiritually necessary.

Letting go of my need for certainty also allowed me to be more honest in the way I approach the Bible. Like many of you, I was raised with the doctrine of *biblical inerrancy*: the belief that the Bible is without error and has one consistent message that never contradicts itself. As neat and tidy as that sounds, no serious critical scholar of the Bible believes this. Evangelical dogma demands it, but it is at odds with the reality of what the Bible is: a very human library of books written by more than forty authors, writing with different purposes, from different cultural perspectives, to different audiences, in three different languages, over several centuries. They do not always agree, and that's okay!

When I was an evangelical, I was constantly frustrated with how badly behaved the Bible was for a book that was supposed to be written by God. We believed it all fit together, but if we were honest, we were often *forcing it to fit*. For example, Paul says: "For by grace you have been saved through faith . . . not a result of works" (Ephesians 2:8–9, ESV). But James says: "A person is justified by works and not by faith alone" (James 2:24, ESV). Anyone can see that this is an obvious contradiction—unless of course they have a preconceived dogmatic belief that the Bible cannot contradict itself.

Many critical scholars who do not wear dogmatic blinders actually believe that James is directly critiquing Paul's theology. They are in conversation with each other, and we get to listen in on their disagreement! What if we found wisdom in the tensions of scripture rather than flattening out the mystery to fit with our doctrinal formulas? The evangelical need for certainty forces these diverse perspectives to agree and fit their doctrinal narrative, but what if ambiguity in the Bible was a feature, not a bug?

This ambiguity is terrifying to evangelicals but historically has been embraced by Judaism. The Talmud, a Jewish holy book, is essentially a collection of thousands of arguments between rabbis, and then further arguments about the arguments! It is a book of disagreements, yet it is considered a holy text because Judaism understands that a diversity of opinions gets us closer to the truth. Certainty is not the goal; wisdom is, and wisdom is often found in the contradictions.

This way of thinking is unfamiliar to evangelicals, but letting go of the need for certainty can be liberating. We are free to continue to change our minds through our lives without the need to figure it out once and for all or land somewhere permanently. The goal is not "knowing the right thing" or even "believing the right thing." Believing the wrong thing won't send you to hell, so you can relax and just focus on believing the *loving* thing. You can focus on living in a way that reflects love for God and your neighbor and makes you feel deeply like your truest self.

Opening up to curiosity is one of my favorite things about realizing that there is no hell. God is not going to punish us for "wrong-think." *We are free to not know.*

It's okay not to be certain about what happens when we die.

It's okay if you don't know exactly what occurred in the spiritual realm at the moment of Jesus's death.

It's okay not to be a Christian at all! You can even be a non-Christian and embrace whichever of Jesus's teachings still speak to you, however you label yourself.

Many of us aren't good at living with uncertainty, because we were raised to think that not knowing meant not believing, which meant we were going to hell. The existence of hell meant that we could not afford to make an intellectually honest inquiry into our beliefs. Doubt was too dangerous. But if we're not permitted to question our beliefs, how can we say we have honestly sought the truth?

There is a Zen Buddhist concept called *beginner's mind*, which is about approaching life with the naivete and wonder of a child. The things we *think we know* can keep us from the delight of learning and discovery, because "in the Beginner's Mind, there are many possibilities, in the expert's, there are few."

Many of us have never approached spiritual questions with the mind of a beginner, because we were told that if we came to the wrong answers, we would be burnt to an eternal crisp. We were required to hold the correct dogmatic belief down to the tiniest detail. It wasn't enough to believe Jesus died on the cross for us; we had to believe in a particular doctrine of substitutionary atonement, or Jesus's sacrifice would not be effective for us. The stakes were so damn high that we had to manufacture certainty about things that *nobody actually knows for sure.*

We don't have to do that anymore. The certainty was never true certainty in the first place. It was fear. In the real world, doubt does not mean damnation. How liberating. Take a moment to breathe deeply and remind yourself that nobody actually knows exactly what happens when we die, and anyone who says they do is manufacturing false certainty—likely because they're afraid. Afraid of not knowing, afraid of what could happen if they aren't certain.

Personally, I have no problem accepting and reciting the Christian creeds, even if some of the language is more metaphorical to me than literal. I receive the creeds as an act of solidarity with two millennia of Christians, but that doesn't mean I can't question or even disagree with them. The wonderful theologian Eugene Rogers says that "Christianity is a language in which to disagree." We can stay in the faith *and* keep our open questions.

Now, Christians don't have an amazing track record of doing this. Before the Council of Nicaea, for example, the exact nature of the divinity of Christ was debated, open to mystery and ambiguity. After that council, the formula of Christ's dual nature as both fully divine and fully human was decided, and dissenters were declared heretics and forced to confess the creed or have their heads lopped off. Violence is not a great way to keep a spirit of curiosity alive!

Now, I can feel that some of you are already struggling with this. Even if we want to ditch the old dogmas, it's tempting to try to replace them with new, better dogmas. We want something solid to believe. In her poem "The World I Live In," Mary Oliver says that many of us are "locked in the orderly house of reasons and proofs" and nudges us to ask, "What's wrong with *Maybe*?" *Maybe* wasn't an answer many of us were allowed to give. Hell didn't leave a lot of room for maybe. As a result, we're not at all accustomed to the discomfort of sitting with maybe. But I've come to believe that we must let go of our need for certainty if we're going to discover a healthy spirituality.

Jesus helps me with this. He made it very simple when he said the entire scripture is summed up in the commands to love God and to love your neighbor as yourself. That's one thing we *can* be certain of. We have that as a firm foundation. But the foundation is in loving behaviors, not in dogmatic beliefs.

It is to love God: find yourself connected to the loving divine presence that infuses all of reality.

It is to love your neighbor: see that loving presence in everyone God puts in our path.

And it is to love yourself, because you bear the divine image, and getting in touch with your divine self is a necessary act of love. There is only one you, so what makes you bloom is holy.

How we live and love matters more than specific dogmatic beliefs, not just because it is impossible to have true certainty around metaphysical theological ideas but also because this is what Jesus himself said was the most important aspect of spirituality.

We can continue to explore these theological and spiritual questions till the day we die, and we may never end up any more certain of anything than we are now, and that would be just fine, especially if along the way we become more loving. Whatever happens when I die, I want a spirituality that helps me love God, others, and myself *while I'm alive*.

And we're not going to be punished for not knowing the unknowable.

AN EXERCISE IN LISTENING TO YOURSELF

As I was writing this chapter, I received a text from my friend Chris, who had just gotten into an argument with her conservative father about religion. Although she left the evangelical church some time ago, she wrote, "Ugh, fucking religious trauma is so real. He just can't understand me anymore, and it triggers my fear of hell." Many of us resonate with this. We think we've left that fear-based belief in the dustbin, but when we're confronted with our dogmatic past, we find that we wonder, "Could I be going to hell?"

In his book *The Four Agreements*, Don Miguel Ruiz says that we all make "agreements" with beliefs, often from a very young age: "As children, we didn't have the opportunity to choose our beliefs, but we *agreed* with the information that was passed to us." We live out the beliefs that we have made agreements with, and these can have positive or negative effects in our life. Many of us agree with negative beliefs, such as "I'm not pretty enough" or "I should be more successful."

For those of us who were taught to believe in hell, *agreeing with that belief has shaped our spirituality*. If you live out a fear-based spirituality for many years, it can leave an impression on your mind that is difficult to erase. Ruiz puts it this way: "We make an agreement with ourselves, and we practice that agreement until it becomes a whole mastery." Just as years of tire tracks leave deep indentations in a dirt road, our hearts bear the grooves of the beliefs we have agreed with and gone on to practice, sometimes for many years. For many of us, our spirituality is deeply marked with fear.

With that in mind, I want us to take an honest inventory of what we have believed about hell and how it has affected us. This is an exercise in discernment and in listening to yourself, but if it helps you to think of it in biblical terms, think of it like this: Jesus teaches, "By their fruit you will recognize them. . . . A good tree cannot bear bad fruit, and a bad tree cannot bear good fruit" (Matthew 7:16, 18). What fruit has belief in hell born in your life? I want to give you a tool for interrogating a belief—for judging its fruit.

For some of you, this will be your least favorite part of the whole book. You may find it all to be woo-woo bullshit and accuse me of leaning on my feelings rather than objective truth. That's totally fine. For others of you, it will be an important, maybe even revolutionary, step from fear into freedom. Either way, I hope you will take a moment to give this work a try.

In her book *Loving What Is: Four Questions That Can Change Your Life*, Byron Katie teaches a helpful method for investigating our thoughts and beliefs. In her view, a belief is a thought that we keep having and that we have attached to. As I've talked with people who are in the process of deconstructing hell, I've noticed that even when they reject the idea of hell intellectually, in the sense that Katie means it, they still "believe in it." Hell is still shaping their notions about God, other people, and themselves. At the time of this writing, it's been seven years since I rejected belief in hell, and yet I find that many of my spiritual thoughts are still shaped by exclusion, binary thinking, fear, and punishment avoidance. Deep grooves don't smooth out easily.

Katie proposes four questions, which she calls "The Work," for inquiring into our beliefs. You can use these four questions on all kinds of beliefs. For example, you may have the thought "My ex is a liar." There may or may not be some objective truth in that statement, but is it a belief that is serving you? Or is it keeping you trapped in a story that is hurting you? This is why we must inquire into our beliefs, whether they're about our interpersonal relationships or the doctrine of hell.

Here are Katie's four questions (with some additions from me):

1. Is it true? (Yes or no. If no, move to question 3.)

2. Can you *absolutely* know that it's true? (Yes or no.)

3. How do you react (and what happens in your body) when you have that thought?

4. Who or what would you be without that thought?

Before you use this method on the topic of hell, let's walk through a more ordinary example, using the negative thought I mentioned earlier: "My ex is a liar." Plenty of people who have gone through a breakup or divorce have had this thought about their ex. It's a very common thought, but possibly an unhelpful one. Before we accept it, it's at least worth investigating.

Let's start with the first question: *Is it true?* This question is supposed to be answered by your gut. What gut reaction rises up to meet the question: yes or no? Let's say that in this case, yes, you can think of several examples where your ex lied.

Now the second question: *Can you* absolutely *know that it's true?* Are there any reasonable doubts, or other ways of viewing it? Well, lying requires intent—can you ever know with total certainty what is in someone else's heart or mind? Everyone has told lies before—does that mean they should be identified with the label *liar?* Is it possible that this is an inaccurate way of labeling your ex? Yes, it's possible. So, in this case, no, you do not *absolutely* know that it's true.

The third question: *How do you react when you have the thought that your ex is a liar?* What happens, physically and emotionally? Is this a thought that leads you into peace and greater levels of connection? Perhaps when you believe that your ex is a liar, you begin to dwell on past hurts. You narrate a story in which you're a victim. This belief affects the communication you might still have with your ex because, say, you share a friend group or you're coparenting children. It causes you to interpret your ex's actions through a negative lens and fail to give them the benefit of the doubt. That is what happens when you believe the thought that your ex is a liar.

The final question is *Who or what would you be without the thought?* In this case, perhaps the belief leads to pain and disconnection with your ex, your children, and/or your mutual friends. So *without* the thought, maybe you're able to show up without cynicism. Without fear. With an open heart, ready to love and listen.

After you investigate the thought with the four questions, Katie encourages you to "turn it around." When we turn a thought around, we give ourselves the opportunity to try on a different thought and see how it feels. Some of us are stuck in bad thoughts about God, ourselves, and other people, and we've made agreements with these thoughts that make them very difficult to change. Changing our beliefs happens one thought at a time. If we want to move away from fear-based beliefs into beliefs that help us live in greater levels of love and connection, these "turnarounds" are one helpful path toward new and better thoughts.

So if the original thought is "My ex is a liar," a turnaround might be "My ex tells the truth." When we turn the thought around, Katie encourages us to look for ways that the new thought is *just as true or even truer* than the original thought. Even if you can think of examples of your ex lying, you can probably also think of many ways they've told the truth. You might also turn it around by saying, "*I* have been a liar," which may not be a perspective you want to fully embrace, but sitting with the ways that it could be considered true may give you some humility in future interactions. When we turn a thought around, it's good to explore various ways alternative truths may fit us better.

Now, I want you to take a few minutes and use Katie's four questions on what you believe (or grew up believing) about hell.

Write a version of your belief in hell, and then interrogate it. Perhaps you'll do an inquiry on the statement "My friends and family who don't believe in Jesus are going to hell." Or

"Unless I'm truly saved, God will send me to hell." Or even "Unless my children are born again, they will go to hell." I strongly encourage you to write down your answers or, at the very least, come up with a concrete answer for each question.

Here is what the four questions might sound like for the thought "Unless I'm truly saved, God will send me to hell." The first question: *Is it true?* You might think, Yes, I have been taught for most of my life that it was true, so perhaps it is.

The second question: *Can you* absolutely *know that it's true?* The answer: Of course not. This is not the kind of thing anybody can absolutely know for sure. Even if there was a rock-solid biblical case for hell (and there isn't), that still couldn't prove it beyond a reasonable doubt.

The third question: *How do you react when you have the thought "Unless I'm truly saved, God will send me to hell"?* For me, that thought makes me feel distant and afraid of God, and causes me to think of God as something other than love. It makes me worry I haven't done enough, am not good enough, don't believe the right things. It is an anxious reaction that does not lead to the fruit of the Spirit or cause me to love like Jesus loves.

The final question: *Who or what would you be without the thought?* Personally, I'd be free to love and be loved by God. Free to love myself without worrying if I measure up. Free to love others without needing to change them. This is what this book is about, and what I want for you if you are reading it.

As a last step, after completing the four questions, think about the statement you began with, and turn it around. Try several variations of these turnarounds. Do any of them feel truer than your original statement? As you say the opposite statements, do you feel internal resistance? It's okay if you do, and it's normal to feel resistance to truths that oppose beliefs that we have agreed with for a long time. Here are some turnaround statements that I've personally found help-ful: "Jesus would not send my friends and family to hell." "God loves me and would never send me to hell." "My chil-dren do not deserve to go to hell." All of these statements now feel far truer to me than the original statements.

If you found this whole exercise silly or trivial, that's fine—feel free to move along. But if you find yourself thinking about it a few days or weeks from now, you can always come back to Katie's four questions. For many of us who have agreed with a spirituality of hell for the majority of our lives, it will take time and work to replace those beliefs with better ones.

New and better beliefs happen one thought at a time. The good news is, you can listen to the love that is inside you. First John 2:21 says, "I do not write to you because you do not know the truth, but because you do know it." Richard Rohr points out that John is speaking of "an implanted knowing in each of us." This is what we are listening for. For some of us, trusting our own inner voice will be scary. We're not used to stepping into our own spiritual authority. But as Rohr says, "How can a person who does not trust himself know how to trust at all?"

In part III of this book, I'm going to talk about the life, mission, death, and resurrection of Jesus. I'm going to unpack what I think the heart of Jesus's message was all about and re-imagine the Christian story without punishment at the center. But I'm not going to reformulate all of Christian doctrine. I will leave many questions unanswered. I don't have all the answers myself! My hope is that the possibilities I present in the Christian story will offer a more loving foundation for your spirituality than the spirituality of hell. I hope that, along with me, you'll learn to dwell in the uncertainty and move forward one new, unfamiliar but beautiful thought at a time.

Part III

A Spirituality of Love

9.

THE BELOVED COMMUNITY

*If There's No Hell,
What's the Point of Jesus's Life?*

God's kingdom is not a place, but a condition. When people are right with each other and with God, they are in the kingdom.

—Howard Thurman

Now that we've looked at how the doctrine of hell makes a healthy spirituality impossible, and now that we've deconstructed the concept of hell from both biblical and nonbiblical perspectives, let's talk about reimagining a new Christian spirituality out from under the shadow of hell. If you've spent most of your life being told the entire point of Christianity is avoiding hell, then it's natural to wonder: If you don't believe in hell, what's the point of being a Christian? If there is no hell, why did Jesus live? Why did Jesus die? What does it mean to be saved? Does any of it mean anything at all?

I think it does. In fact, I think the message of Jesus matters even more when you take hell out of the equation, and over the course of the next few chapters I'll explain why.

I know not everyone agrees with me. I recently received a comment on social media that said, "If you don't think hell is real and you claim to follow Christ, what do you even think Christ does for you? If there is no hell to be saved from, why do we need a savior?"

Being a cheeky little jackass, I decided to turn the question around on him, saying, "I'd actually encourage you to think for a moment and ask yourself what Christ does for *you* if there is no hell. Because if that's all it is, does that not strike you as a deficient sort of faith? Or is saving you from hell the only good reason you can think of for Jesus to be worth following?"

He did not appreciate this response, but to me, it illustrates just how empty most conservative Christian spirituality really is. If you take hell away, what's left? If you remove the negative from your spirituality, is there anything positive or constructive there?

For me, following Jesus is something positive in and of itself, not just a way to avoid something negative. I believe Jesus offers us so much more than a get-out-of-hell-free card. I believe Jesus shows us how to connect with God, ourselves, and other people in this life and for the sake of the world.

WHY DID JESUS LIVE?

Judging from the way that many Christians talk about Jesus, you'd think Jesus did not need to live at all. He only needed to die. Most Christian denominations teach some version of the idea that Jesus's death was a payment to God for their sins, to save us from hell. If hell is at stake, nothing in the life of Jesus could possibly eclipse the importance of the death of Jesus. This is unfortunate, because few people have lived lives as compelling and extraordinary as Jesus's. Few lives could teach us more! And yet, a spirituality of hell will never center on the lessons we learn from the *life* of Jesus; it will obsessively fixate on his death as a ticket out of hell.

This is a loss for Christianity, and a loss for the world. Our world could certainly use several billion people deeply imitating the life of Jesus Christ, regardless of what they believed about the supernatural effects of his death. The earliest Christians called their faith not Christianity but *the Way*, because to them it was a *way of living in the world* rather than a set of beliefs. Many conservative Christians would say that I no longer qualify as a Christian because I am agnostic about several historic doctrines and believe several others to be more metaphorical than literal. However, I have no intention of abandoning the label *Christian*, because to be a Christian has always first meant to follow the way of Jesus.

Many Christians, feeling they've secured salvation from hell through the saving death of Jesus, build their entire spirituality around convincing other people to agree with them about how Jesus's death can save them from hell also. For them, spirituality looks like becoming a better witness for Christ, telling your neighbors about Christ, and tithing to your church so they can put on events to reach your neighbors for Christ. The point of their Christian lives is to save people from hell, by getting everyone to agree with them in their beliefs about Jesus.

There is a major problem with this: It doesn't look or feel anything like the spirituality of Jesus.

Evangelicalism has traded the spirituality *of* Jesus for a belief system *about* Jesus. If we want to learn why Jesus lived, we should look first at Jesus's life, not at his death. Thankfully, we do not have to scratch our heads and wonder what Jesus lived for or what he was passionate about. Jesus tells us, explicitly.

JESUS'S PURPOSE, ACCORDING TO JESUS

In Luke 4, Jesus kicks off his ministry with a dramatic sermon in which he announces what he's going to do. Spoiler alert: His mission is not to save people for the afterlife. It is a revolution of love and liberation in this life.

If you're familiar with the gospels, you know that they are often short on description; the gospel writers jump from story to story with few narrative details. But scholars point out that this story in Luke's Gospel is given special prominence: Time slows down as Luke narrates every move Jesus makes.

Jesus stands.

A scroll is handed to him.

He unrolls it.

This wealth of details indicates that Luke wants us to know that this is one of the most important moments in his book.

Jesus stands and reads aloud this passage from the book of Isaiah:

> *The Spirit of the Lord is upon me,*
> *because he has anointed me*
> *to proclaim good news to the poor.*
>
> *He has sent me to proclaim liberty to the captives*
> *and recovering of sight to the blind,*
> *to set at liberty those who are oppressed,*
> *to proclaim the year of the Lord's favor.*
>
> Luke 4:18–19, ESV

Jesus rolls the scroll back up.

He sits down.

Then he announces, "Today this scripture is fulfilled in your hearing" (Luke 4:21).

This is a mic drop moment. Jesus tells us *what he came to do* and *who he came to do it for*.

What he came to *do* is bring liberation. This liberation is spiritual, but it is also material. The "year of the Lord's favor" in the passage from Isaiah that Jesus reads is a part of Jewish law, also known as the Jubilee year. Every fifty years, the people of Israel were supposed to "proclaim liberty throughout the land"—not from sin, but from material injustice and inequality (Leviticus 25:10). It was an economic reset. Wealth and land were to be redistributed. Every debt was to be canceled. Slaves were to be set free. Jesus says that this is the promise that will be fulfilled in his message and ministry. Jesus brings good news for *this life*, not just the afterlife— good news for all of human society, not just individual souls.

Jesus also tells us who he came *for*: the poor, the captives, the blind, and the oppressed. Jesus came for the people on the bottom, the people who were left out. This is a pattern in Jesus's life. In his Sermon on the Plain in Luke 6, Jesus lists the poor, the hungry, those who weep, and those who are persecuted as the truly blessed ones. In Luke 14:13, he tells his disciples to "invite the poor, the crippled, the lame, the blind" to their feasts rather than the rich. Jesus tells us that his purpose is to go to the marginalized and bring about social reversal and liberation.

This is a different vision of Jesus than the Jesus of evangelicalism, who is simply a divine sacrifice that made a way for us to avoid the flames of hell. But if we don't grasp Jesus's purpose *for this world*, not only will we miss out on the heart of Jesus, we will also become exactly the kinds of hypocritical religious people that Jesus's ministry was aligned against.

THE WHITE CHRIST VERSUS THE BLACK CHRIST

If there was any group of Christians that understood the importance of Jesus's mission of liberation for this world, it was the Black Christians enslaved in the American South. In his book *The Spirituals and the Blues*, theologian James Cone explains that in the subversive spirituals sung by enslaved people, "heaven" wasn't only about the next life—it was code for freedom from slavery in the North. When slaves sang, "I am bound for the land of Canaan," they were knowingly referring to Canada. When they sang, "I looked over Jordan and what did I see, coming for to carry me home," they were talking about the Ohio River, and they were dreaming of the deliverance of the Underground Railroad. In other words, "heaven" and "salvation" pointed to the freedom and justice of emancipation in life, not in death.

The white slaveholders had a very different view of salvation, and a very different Christ. In her classic book *The Black Christ*, Kelly Brown Douglas contrasts the white Christ of the slaveholders with the Black Christ of the enslaved. Earlier in this book, we saw how the doctrine of hell enabled and justified colonialism and white supremacy. Nowhere was this more evident than in American slavery. For white, slaveholding Christians, the essence of salvation was believing in Jesus Christ's saving work on the cross. The life of Jesus was not particularly important. What Jesus did in his ministry—healing the sick, preaching good news to the poor, calling the religious elites to account—were not essential aspects of salvation. All that mattered was that Jesus, the God-man, died for our sins so that we could be forgiven and go to heaven when we die. The white Christ did not care about liberation in this world, as long as people believed the correct thing to prepare them for the next world.

Douglas writes that "with salvation guaranteed through belief, white people could be slaveholders and Christian without guilt or fear about the state of their soul." In fact, the slaveholders could even pat themselves on the back, thinking they were doing a good thing when they kidnapped people from Africa, because now these people could learn about the white Christ and go to heaven. As they tore families apart and chained people like animals in the bottom decks of their slave ships, the slaveholders could assure themselves that as long as they were "Christianizing" their slaves, they were doing them a service.

If the Africans remained in their homeland, these white Christians reasoned, they would never hear the gospel. Even the most inhuman forms of slavery could not compare to an eternal future in hell. Their only hope was the gospel message that the white Christians brought to them. Even though a quarter of enslaved people didn't survive the brutal voyage across the Atlantic, white Christian slaveholders could assure themselves that at least they evangelized to those they enslaved, and taught them the scriptures (making sure to focus on the verses like Ephesians 6:5: "Slaves, obey your earthly masters").

If your stomach is churning at the horror of this baptized slaveholder logic, good. It is pure evil. And it is a natural result of the spirituality of hell. For white slaveholders, salvation was disconnected from this world, human history, and the havoc they wreaked on Black lives.

Many enslaved people understandably rejected the Christian message completely, and of course it's impossible to know how many more would have rejected it if they hadn't been forcibly forbidden from practicing their own religions. But one of the great surprises of religious history is that many enslaved people embraced Christianity, because they saw that the Christ of scripture had a very different message than the white Christ of slaveholders.

Douglas explains that enslaved people held secret Christian church services, where they preached a very different kind of Christ. They stressed Jesus's life and ministry to the poor and oppressed of his day. They saw that Jesus was more like them than he was like the slaveholders. The "Black Christ" was on their side. Enslaved people cared about the cross, but not as a magical formula to enable them to go to heaven when they died. For them, the cross was the ultimate proof that God was on their side; in Douglas's words, "through the cross, Jesus's suffering and the slaves' suffering became one."

The Christian faith of enslaved people fueled their fight for freedom in *this* world. Their preaching emphasized the stories of God's liberation in history. Stories like the Exodus, or the Israelites' return out of exile in Babylon. They saw what so many American Christians still struggle to see: If Jesus doesn't matter for *this* life and *this* world, he doesn't matter at all.

The Christ of white evangelicalism is still the white Christ: a disembodied being who cares about saving souls from hell in the next life rather than liberating living people from the hell we create in this life.

IT'S ALL GONNA BURN

This afterlife-focused spirituality continues to shape the way many Christians, particularly evangelicals, view the world and their place in it. I saw this firsthand in my own experiences as an evangelical pastor.

One of my pastoral mentors in evangelicalism was a grizzled man named Tim. He had a habit of constantly muttering vaguely Christian phrases under his breath to himself like mantras, and one of his favorites was "It's all gonna burn." I heard him say it whenever he felt a pang of envy over material possessions. For example, he desperately wanted a Harley-Davidson motorcycle, but it was financially out of reach. When he crossed paths with one in real life, he would shake his head and remind himself, "It's all gonna burn."

This mindset is common in evangelicalism. *This* world is going to burn. It's the *next* world that's important.

Now, I don't want to be too hard on Tim! I think it's a good thing to remind ourselves of the temporary nature of wealth and possessions. Jesus himself says, "Do not lay up for yourselves treasures on earth, where moth and rust destroy . . . but lay up for yourselves treasures in heaven" (Matthew 6:19–20, ESV). But for Jesus, heaven is not a place you go to after you die. Rather, heaven is God's space. It is a spiritual reality, and it is with us and all around us. To lay up treasures in heaven is not about collecting rewards in the afterlife. It is about living for the things of heaven right now. To live for the things that matter most in this world, the things that connect us to love and bring about God's peace.

In a very literal sense, the world is already burning. Global temperatures are rising, increasing the number of wildfires and other weather-related disasters, and potentially posing a threat to human existence as we know it. Yet I was raised being told that climate change was not important, because even if we do experience ecological disaster, Jesus is coming back soon anyway. The theologian Jürgen Moltmann writes that because Christians have reduced salvation to the afterlife and not this life, we have "unconsciously abandoned nature to its disastrous exploitation by human beings." If this world is going to burn, it's because we're letting it burn. We have abandoned the precious earth God created. We have allowed the exploitation of the garden we've been given to tend.

The evangelical response to Trump's return to power in 2024 reveals how dangerous this disengagement from earthly concerns can be. While some evangelical leaders explicitly endorsed Trump, others engaged in spiritual bypassing, using biblical language to avoid confronting real-world consequences. For example, at a popular evangelical church just two days before this pivotal election, I heard the pastor remind his congregation, "Remember where your citizenship fully and finally lies. . . . We are foreigners and strangers on this earth. . . . Every other allegiance will expire." While this may sound spiritual and politically neutral, such vague platitudes actually enable oppression by failing to confront it directly and minimizing the importance of our earthly involvement. When over 80 percent of white evangelicals support a race-baiting, fascist-leaning demagogue, speaking in generalities about "heavenly citizenship" without naming and opposing the hatred in the white reactionary Christian movement essentially endorses it.

Being a "citizen of heaven" is indeed a beautiful metaphor, but it doesn't mean we focus solely on saving souls for the afterlife. It means we are called to represent the values of heaven here on earth. And what that truly means is liberation for the oppressed.

We have a serious problem, and it isn't in heaven—it's on earth. It's in the hospital parking lot where a woman died after being denied miscarriage care due to abortion bans. It's in our schools, where children drill for the mass shootings we've decided are an inevitable part of American life. It's in the children's eyes as they are torn from their families at the border. If our heavenly citizenship doesn't rattle the chains of domination that hang heavy on our brothers and sisters, then it means nothing at all.

Salvation. When you hear this word, what comes to mind? For most of us, it's the afterlife. It is salvation for the next world, not for this world.

But, at the risk of sounding obvious, once you reject the concept of hell, salvation cannot primarily mean going to heaven. Salvation cannot merely be about "who's in" and "who's out" in the next world. Ultimately, one way or another, everybody's in. God will be all in all. So salvation is about "this world," or it doesn't matter at all. For some people, this makes the idea of salvation seem trivial or unnecessary. They might say, "If everybody goes to heaven, salvation is pointless." But that is only true if this world and this life are pointless.

If hell is real, then it's true that this world doesn't matter very much. The suffering of the world is but the blink of an eye compared to everlasting torment. Our lives in this world are a blip compared to eternity. If there is an eternal hell for the unsaved, then the only valuable purpose of this life is to be "saved" to avoid such a fate. This is slaveholder logic, and it has justified every possible evil under the sun.

But this life is not about escaping hell. There is no hell to escape except the hells we create for ourselves and for others. This life matters. This world, and the suffering in this world, matter. Whatever is on the other side of this (and I believe the eternal arms of love are on the other side of this), we only get one shot at this life. The purpose of this life is not to check the right boxes to get in on the good part of the next life. This life is its own purpose.

And I believe we can find that purpose in Jesus. Jesus showed it to us. He called it *the kingdom of God*.

ON EARTH AS IT IS IN HEAVEN

The central message of Jesus was the kingdom of God: "The time is fulfilled, and the kingdom of God has come near; repent, and believe in the good news" (Mark 1:15, NRSV). But the kingdom of God is not heaven. It is about life in this world.

This is not a progressive belief or a fringe interpretation; this is a common understanding of Jesus's central message. The popular evangelical scholar N.T. Wright defines it this way: "The kingdom of God is not about going to heaven when you die. . . . It is about God's passion to redeem and restore his creation, and his insistence on doing so through the work of his image-bearing human beings."

Jesus demonstrated the kingdom of God throughout his whole ministry—his Sermon on the Mount was the State of the Union address for a new kind of world where the last are first. His parables reimagined a world operating on a different set of values that challenged cultural norms. His healing and acts of deliverance pointed to the liberation God desired for all creation. Everything Jesus did and said pointed toward the kingdom, and he gathered a community to embody this vision.

The kingdom of God is a political and religious metaphor about life under the rule of God rather than under the rulers of this world. It is meant to cause us to dream about a day when God is king and Caesar is not. In Jesus's day, the people were ruled by Rome, which was, in the words of theologian Marcus Borg, an "ancient domination system ruled by powerful and wealthy elites." Sound familiar? That's what the kingdoms of this world are always like. They are fueled by violence and defined by oppression. America is not a "Christian nation." America is a domination system ruled by powerful and wealthy elites, just like Rome, just like every kingdom.

The kingdom of God, on the other hand, is God's dream for the world. It is a kingdom of justice, ruled by love. It is what we pray for whenever we pray the most famous Christian prayer, the Lord's Prayer, taught by Jesus to his disciples: "Thy kingdom come, thy will be done, on earth as it is in heaven." The prayer is not for us to go to heaven. The prayer is for God's dream for the world to come to earth.

And after we pray for God's kingdom to come on earth, Jesus taught us to pray for two specific examples: "Give us this day our daily bread, and forgive us our debts, as we also have forgiven our debtors." These two petitions reveal something of the priority of the kingdom: that it is good news for the poor. Jesus was speaking to a peasant class. Food scarcity and indebtedness were two major survival problems they dealt with. Having enough food was not guaranteed. Amazingly, this is still a severe problem. Even in the richest country in the history of the world, one in five children across America doesn't have enough to eat. We know from the Lord's Prayer that God's kingdom is about *everyone having enough*.

Although this prayer is recorded in Luke 11:4 as saying, "Forgive us our sins," the version in Matthew 6:12 says, "Forgive us our debts." It's likely that both meanings were intended by Jesus. In his day, there was massive wealth inequality between rich landowners and poor day laborers. For the already poor, indebtedness could lead to servitude. Our world has not changed much. During the COVID-19 pandemic, the wealth of the top 1 percent increased by $6.5 trillion, while the bottom half of households collectively lost $232 billion over the same period. Meanwhile, household debt is at record highs. But in God's kingdom, debts are forgiven and God's children "let no debt remain outstanding, except the continuing debt to love one another, for whoever loves others has fulfilled the law" (Romans 13:8).

Our world is structured to serve the powerful, but the kingdom of God is about building a new world, a world that works for everyone, especially the poor.

Many conservative Christians do not believe it is the job of the church or Christians to build a better world. They scoff at "utopian thinking." They call progressive ideas naive and idealistic, and say that because we're all sinners, the world is unlikely to change for the better. And yet, we know that people have changed the world for the better in many ways, often as a part of their Christian faith. Abolitionists were called naive and idealistic for wanting to abolish slavery, but they fought for a better world. Suffragettes were laughed off for wanting equal rights for women, but they fought for a better world. Social Gospel Christians in Canada were called impractical for wanting universal health care, but now universal health care is normative throughout the developed world—except in America, where many conservative Christians still call it idealistic and impossible. I believe these have been movements of God's Spirit in history.

The end of segregation in our country was seen as a utopian pipe dream, but following the Spirit of God, the civil rights movement ultimately triumphed over Jim Crow. The advance of LGBTQ rights is another liberative move of the Spirit. God's kingdom is advancing, and the Spirit is still setting at liberty those who are oppressed. The question is, Which side are we on? Some Christians have too often been *against* the movement of the Spirit for a more just world, but there have always been those—Christian and non-Christian—who have joined Jesus in working to see God's dream for the world come to light.

People sometimes ask me if I still believe in demons, post-deconstruction. I don't see why not. The earth is under the control of systems of oppression. That's the secular way to say demons exist. Paul would say it this way: "We do not wrestle against flesh and blood, but against the rulers, against the authorities, against the cosmic powers over this present darkness" (Ephesians 6:12, ESV).

Biblical language often personifies structural forces. This spiritual language can be unhelpful if it causes us to think it is only talking about the afterlife, and not the flesh-and-blood oppressive realities of this life, but it can be powerful if it causes us to remember that the struggle for flourishing in this world is a spiritual struggle, and that God cares about this world and dismantling the oppressive powers within it. White supremacy, sexism, ableism, the patriarchy, queerphobia, climate-change denial, capitalism—these are some of the domination systems that rule the kingdoms of this world. These systems crucify people, especially people at the bottom of the hierarchy, just as these kinds of systems always have.

Jesus showed us a new way to live in the world, under the reign of God's love, not under the tyranny of domination systems. I love how the haunting Christmas hymn "O Holy Night" puts it:

> *Truly He taught us to love one another;*
> *His law is love and His Gospel is Peace.*
> *Chains shall He break, for the slave is our brother,*
> *And in His name, all oppression shall cease.*

In some ways, the kingdom of God is the flip side of the message of Gehenna. When we reject the vision of the kingdom Jesus offers us, the result is Gehenna: the natural consequences of our failures to love, reflecting back onto us and those around us. Gehenna is where the demonic powers of domination in this world lead. The kingdom of God is where love leads.

THE KIN-DOM OF GOD

The kingdom of God does things very differently than the kingdoms of this world. Jesus says, "If my kingdom were of this world, my servants would have been fighting. . . . But my kingdom is not from the world" (John 18:36, ESV). The kingdoms of this world are fueled by violence. Jesus's kingdom is not *from* the world, but it is *for* the world.

The mujerista* theologian Ada María Isasi-Díaz coined the expression "the kin-dom of God" to emphasize the fundamental difference in how God's kingdom is meant to operate. In God, we are *kin*. We are family.

In the kingdoms of this world, we are often striving for our own advancement, or the advancement of our racial or social group. Kingdoms have hierarchies: rulers and subjects. The kin-dom of God, in contrast, is interconnected and interdependent. We are not strangers or competitors; we are brothers and sisters. In God's kin-dom, as in a family, we are not content with extreme inequalities. We stand in solidarity with others against systems of oppression, like racism, sexism, and economic exploitation, because we recognize that what hurts one of us hurts all of us.

I have seen a beautiful example of kin-dom in the queer community. So many of my queer friends have been rejected or disowned by their biological families. As painful as that loss is, there is something particularly beautiful about the community of "chosen family" that can grow on the other side of that rejection. All queer people have some experience of marginalization. Even those whose families fully accept them have still faced forms of discrimination throughout their lives. As a result, the queer community has a superpower when it comes to including outsiders.

I have experienced this firsthand. Back when I was a pastor, I found community inside my church family. My church family were the people who helped us move and brought us meals after our children were born. When I left my position as a pastor, I lost that network of support. I also moved from a rural coastal town in North Carolina to Raleigh, a midsize

---

* Mujerista theology is a form of liberation theology that emphasizes the perspectives of Latina women; *mujer* is Spanish for "woman."

city, and I found that making friends in a new city was challenging.

But then a gay friend there invited me to join a queer kickball team. There was already a Brian on the team, so they called me "straight Brian," and I was perfectly fine being the minority for once in my life. I was so impressed by the nonjudgmental, radical acceptance of this community. They made me feel like I could be fully myself. It was so refreshing that I realized I may have never experienced that before. Our games were on Sundays, after church. I felt that on those days, I went to church twice.

A safe space, where you can be loved just as you are, where you can experience your own belovedness, is what we all long for. It's what God wants for us. It's what I want to create for others. It's what the kingdom of God is all about: connected to oneself, to others, and to God.

The evangelical church attempts to offer this kind of community, but there are always limits on who can be included. It's "inclusion with an asterisk." To truly belong, you have to conform to evangelical beliefs, especially around sexual orientation. Gay people in nonaffirming churches are expected to remain celibate and cannot experience the romantic partnerships that straight Christians take for granted.

Yet the nature of the kin-dom of God is to always be breaking down exclusionary boundaries, welcoming more people into the family. The borders are always extending, the community always widening. The radical inclusivity I experienced in the queer community echoes Jesus's own teachings on the expansive nature of neighborly love. In Luke 10:29, a religious authority who "wanted to justify himself" confronted Jesus, asking, "And who is my neighbor?" As so many of us are, he was looking to narrow his concern to his own group. But Jesus doesn't let us do that. He responded with the parable of the good Samaritan, which *universalized the definition of neighbor* to include even despised people groups. Yet most evangelical churches would not welcome in my kickball teammates as neighbors the way those teammates welcomed me.

Martin Luther King Jr. preached a beautiful sermon on this parable, which I believe captures the heart of the kindom of God:

> *Too seldom do we see people in their true humanness. . . . We fail to think of them as fellow human beings made from the same basic stuff as we, molded in the same divine image. . . . The good neighbor looks beyond the external accidents and discerns those inner qualities that make all men human and, therefore, brothers.*

King concludes his sermon like this:

> *No longer can we afford the luxury of passing by on the other side. Such folly was once called moral failure; today it will lead to universal suicide. We cannot long survive spiritually separated in a world that is geographically together. In the final analysis, I must not ignore the wounded man on life's Jericho Road, because he is a part of me and I am a part of him. His agony diminishes me, and his salvation enlarges me.*

The community King dreamed about demanded that we see our connectedness, our oneness. What Jesus called the kingdom of God, King called "the beloved community": a world of racial equality, economic justice, and global solidarity. Like Jesus, King sought to extend the definition of neighbor, so that all people would be valued as image bearers of

God, brothers and sisters in one human family. King fought for this dream, knowing that he would not see it in his lifetime but that God's dream for the world would ultimately prevail: "The end is reconciliation; the end is redemption; the end is the creation of the Beloved Community."

Like Jesus, King was executed by "the powers." This should not surprise us; it's what domination systems always do to the love that threatens their power.

That is never the end of the story, though. Domination systems build crosses. But God raises the dead.

The life, mission, and passion of Jesus beckon us to join him in seeking the renewal of *this* world. His vision invites us to look for opportunities to extend radical acceptance to those who are marginalized or excluded, like what I experienced on my queer kickball team. This is what it means to make Jesus Lord. It's not about praying a salvation prayer to secure our mansion in heaven. It's about rejecting the powers of this world and giving our faith—our allegiance—to the way of Jesus, the way of love and liberation.

Many Christians believe that the kingdom of God is both "already" and "not yet." In other words, they believe that we see the kingdom in glimpses now, but one day God will break in and decisively make this world what it's supposed to be. They call this the "second coming." I think that would be beautiful, but I can't say for sure if that's going to happen or not. I'm not sure what God is going to do in the future. What I do know is what we're supposed to do right now.

Jesus told us that he would come to us, not just a second time, but every day, in "the least of these." Kurt Marti, a Swiss pastor and poet, prayed, "The ones we would rather not see are Your gaze. The ones we would rather not hear are Your voice." Many Christians, in looking for a second coming of Christ, miss the way that Christ comes to us again and again in the face of the poor. We know what God's dream for the world looks like—Jesus showed us—so we can continue Jesus's kin-dom work right now in our world, creating beloved communities where all are welcomed and our boundaries are ever-widening.

This vision of spirituality we get from Jesus is so different from the spirituality of hell. The spirituality of hell is obsessed with being right and with convincing other people to believe like we believe. But Jesus didn't try to convince people of any doctrines. Instead, Jesus shows us how connected we are, even to people who believe differently from us. If this sounds terribly simple, you're right. It is a simple message, but hell has twisted it. Fear and punishment have blinded us to the simplicity of love. The spirituality of Jesus isn't complicated, but it is difficult, demanding, and dangerous—so dangerous that the world killed him for it. And, as we'll see in the next chapter, that death can have immense meaning for us, even when we don't believe in hell.

10.

JESUS CHRIST, EXECUTED ENEMY OF THE STATE

*If There's No Hell,
What's the Point of Jesus's Death?*

When American Christians realize that they can meet Jesus only in the crucified bodies in our midst, they will encounter the real scandal of the cross.

—James Cone

The cross is perhaps the most recognizable religious image in the world and is the central symbol of Christianity. And yet, for many of us, it is very difficult to separate it from a spirituality of hell. The story of the cross we learned is a story of punishment.

When I asked my social media followers to share with me how the cross currently fits into their spirituality, they responded with answers like these:

The cross seems morbid and honestly inappropriate to teach kids about.

The only thing I can think of is the amount of suffering that Jesus was willing to endure for love. But even that is hard to figure out . . . it just sits weird at the moment.

The cross is used as torture porn to emotionally manipulate others into feeling terrible and shameful.

I once heard a pastor say it's the equivalent of making a hangman's noose the symbol of your movement, which I think he meant to say was very powerful and shocking to see, but it was not the flex he thought it was.

I have a cross tattooed on my chest and honestly these days it feels like a scarlet letter.

It reminds me that the state will always be against liberation, especially if it's your spirit that's free.

I see it as a brutal murder to satisfy the need to punish someone.

Abusive. All the time I spent as a kid thinking about this man who was tortured "because of me."

This confusion over what to make of the cross is very understandable to me. In my upbringing, as in so many other people's, the cross was the center of the story about a punishing God. When the cross was discussed, the central message was that my personal, individual sin put Jesus on the cross. He hung there *for* me and *because* of me. Because of my sin. "It was my sin that held him there," as one popular hymn said.

This view of the cross has everything to do with hell. Tim Keller was not known as a hellfire preacher, but even he explained it this way:

Unless we come to grips with [hell], we will never even begin to understand the depths of what Jesus did for us on the cross. His body was being destroyed in the worst possible way, but that was a flea bite compared to what was happening to his soul. When he cried out that his God had forsaken him he was experiencing hell itself. But consider—if our debt for sin is so great that it is never paid off there, but our hell stretches on for eternity, then what are we to conclude from the fact that Jesus said the payment was "finished" (John 19:30) after only three hours? We learn that what he felt on the cross was far worse and deeper than all of our deserved hells put together.

Almost every hymn I sang growing up confirmed this story. Jesus paid for our sins. We deserved hell, but Jesus went through hell *for us*, on the cross. If we believe in him, then our record of sin is placed on Jesus's account, in a divine transaction, so that God's punishment lands on Jesus instead of on us. (It remains unclear to me why Jesus's payment only works if we believe in it, since the Bible says repeatedly that Jesus died for the sins of the whole world,* but that part about individual belief was always considered very important. Anyone who didn't *believe* in Jesus's sacrifice on the cross would suffer for their sins in hell.)

This concept is often called *penal substitutionary atonement*. Different Christian denominations espouse slightly different versions of this school of thought, with slightly different names. I will simply call it the *payment theory* of the cross. The cross was a payment for our sins, to a wrathful God. For many Christians, this story *is* the gospel. But it's not very good news, and it doesn't actually fit very well with the mission of Jesus or the God of the Bible.

First of all, the payment theory is a message about the afterlife, not about this life. Jesus longed to see the kingdom of God "on earth, as it is in heaven" (Matthew 6:10), but if his true purpose was to save souls for the next world, then this world doesn't matter very much at all.

Second, it's a message that has nothing to do with the priorities of Jesus's earthly mission. Jesus's passion—which he called the kingdom of God—was to transform the world into a world of love and welcome for the least of these. Dying as a payment to a wrathful God is completely disconnected from Jesus's stated mission.

Third, in this theory, the cross changes God rather than

---

* See 1 John 2:2, Hebrews 2:9, John 3:16, and chapter 7 of this book.

us. I do believe that the cross is about change and transformation, but I believe it is about *our* transformation, not God's. This story teaches that God was angry with and disconnected from us because of our sins, but when Jesus moved some numbers around on God's cosmic ledger, God was able to be in relationship with us again. The payment of the cross transforms God's posture toward us from wrath to love rather than transforming *our* posture toward God and others. This does not reflect the God of the Bible, who is always there for us—whose "steadfast love . . . never ceases" (Lamentations 3:22, NRSV) and who is "an ever-present help in [times of] trouble" (Psalm 46:1). The story of the payment theory shapes a spirituality of separation, not connection.

Finally, I think it's important to note that this theory was not fully taught until the year 1100 by a theologian named Anselm of Canterbury. In Anselm's day, feudal lords demanded payment when their honor was besmirched, so it makes sense that was the metaphor he used to describe God: Humanity's sin offended God's honor, someone had to pay for it, and Jesus did so by dying on the cross. But just because a metaphor is useful to people in one time and place doesn't mean it's universally true. For the first millennium of the church, nobody believed this story about the cross, yet today, many Christians say that if you don't believe it, you do not have "saving faith" in Jesus and you're destined for hell. By that logic, every Christian for the first thousand years of the church is in hell. I don't buy it.

SACRIFICE: A SUBVERSIVE METAPHOR, NOT A LITERAL PAYMENT

So if Jesus didn't die to pay for our sins, why does the New Testament refer to his death as a sacrifice? This language does show up in several places, for example, Hebrews 7:27 (ESV): "He has no need, like those high priests, to offer sacrifices daily, first for his own sins and then for those of the people, since he did this once for all when he offered up himself." Sacrifice is a beautiful and powerful metaphor, but like many metaphors, when it is pressed too far into wooden literalism, it becomes toxic. Seeing Jesus as a "sacrifice" for sin does not imply that God is a bloodthirsty war god that demands a victim. When we make Jesus a *literal* sacrifice rather than a *metaphorical* one, it creates an ugly story and an ugly God.

Remember, the first people wrestling with the meaning of the cross were first-century Jews, whose religious life revolved around the Temple in Jerusalem and the sacrificial system. According to the religious laws of the time, you had to sacrifice certain animals or foods to God in order to give thanks for certain blessings, atone for certain sins, and so on. These sacrifices couldn't be done by anyone, anywhere. They had to be performed by priests at the Temple in Jerusalem. Thus access to God was mediated through the Temple and religious authorities.

Jesus directly subverts this system, telling the religious leaders who uphold it, "Go and learn what this means: 'I desire mercy, not sacrifice'" (Matthew 9:13). Seeing Jesus as a "once-and-for-all" sacrifice is a subversive metaphor. Rather than establishing punishment or sacrifice as central to spirituality, it teaches us there are *no religious requirements* to access the reality of the divine.

This is why the three synoptic Gospels (Matthew, Mark, and Luke) tell us that at the moment of Jesus's death, the curtain in the inner sanctum of the Temple was torn from top to bottom. You may have been taught that this meant that we could only be in relationship with a holy God because God's

166 - HELL BENT

wrath was satiated by Jesus's death. That's not what it means. The torn veil is a rebuke of any system that says some people are in and some people are out. The metaphor of Jesus as a sacrifice means that you can't gatekeep God, because God "is not far from any one of us" (Acts 17:27).

Theologian Marcus Borg points out that the Temple system "claimed an institutional monopoly on access to God" and that "it is therefore ironic to realize that the religion that formed around Jesus would within four hundred years begin to claim for itself an institutional monopoly on grace and access to God." By making Christianity all about who gets into heaven and who doesn't, we have inverted the grace of the gospel and turned it into just another way to gatekeep God.

Jesus's death offers us a message of radical grace. According to this way of looking at the sacrificial metaphor, you are not "saved" because Jesus's blood paid a literal sin-debt to God. You are saved by recognizing that God accepts you fully and no sacrifice was ever needed. God did not need to change. Being "saved" is having our eyes open to this truth: You are already forgiven. God is already with you.

JESUS DIED FOR WHAT JESUS LIVED FOR

At this point, you may be asking: If God didn't need Jesus to die as a form of payment for our sins, then why *did* Jesus die?

Well, first of all, Jesus did not just *die*. That makes it sound like he got cancer, or passed away peacefully in bed. Jesus was *killed*. More accurately, he was *executed*. Most specifically, he was *crucified*. A crucifixion was a political death. It was a very specific method of execution used by the Roman Empire to make a public spectacle of anyone who would dare defy their power.

One of Paul's favorite terms for Jesus is "Christ crucified." After hearing this kind of language over and over our whole lives, we're desensitized to it, but it would not have been a banal cliché to his audience at all. They would have heard that expression as something more like "Christ, executed enemy of the state." Jesus died a political death because Jesus preached a political message; his message was about the way the world *should be*, which means it was also a critique of the way the world *was*. Jesus proclaimed the kingdom of God as an alternative to Rome and the other kingdoms of the world. It was an indictment of the people in charge. Jesus said their way was going to lead to Gehenna—to destruction.

Here's a pretty badass thing about Christianity that we don't talk about enough: Jesus is the only major religious figure to be executed as an enemy of the state. When we talk about the significance of Jesus's death, shouldn't that matter?

If Jesus only died as a substitute for God's punishment against sin, then Jesus did not have to be killed as a political agitator fighting for a better world. If the death of Jesus is primarily the story of individual souls being saved from hell, then the message that got him killed—his passion for the kingdom of God—is not necessary at all. If we fail to acknowledge the political connotations of Jesus's death, then we hamstring his message. The dream that Jesus lived for was the dream that Jesus died for. Jesus died for the world— *for the world to be transformed.*

In order to better anchor the death of Jesus in his real-world struggle, I have found it helpful to notice the many parallels between Jesus and revolutionary figures like Martin Luther King Jr. Like Jesus, King died for the dream he lived for. King's dream of "the beloved community" echoed many of the same ideas from Jesus's "kingdom of God." In his struggle for this dream, King found incredible solace and spiritual power in the symbol of the cross. In his collection of sermons, *Strength to Love*, just about every sermon mentions it. But King did not have a punitive vision of the cross. The cross did not make King afraid of a wrathful God. Instead, it gave him strength to love.

As this chapter explores what Jesus's death means without the specter of hell looming behind it, I do not want you to feel pressure to reclaim the cross as a spiritual symbol. If it was weaponized against you, it may be painful, and you may be better served by other spiritual symbols and ideas. But if you are able to bravely receive it, I believe the cross can be a great spiritual resource in helping connect you to God, others, and yourself. Here are four ways the cross still powerfully speaks to me.

GOD IS ON THE SIDE OF LIBERATION

Christians believe that we encounter something unique, important, and surprising about the nature of God in the cross of Jesus Christ. I think the first thing we learn, very simply, is what God wants from us—what God says *yes* to.

Crucifying people isn't what God does; it's what the rulers of this world do. By putting Jesus on the cross, the powers of domination said an emphatic *no* to the kingdom of God. They say no to inclusion for all people, no to centering the marginalized, no to valuing people over religious dogmas, and no to lifting up the poor and letting the last be first. They said no to liberation.

But the cross is not the end of the story. Three days later, an empty tomb *vindicated* the mission of Jesus. Because no matter what the Roman Empire said about Jesus's mission, God said yes. Living the way of Jesus may not lead to success under the powers of this world, but the resurrection is God's stamp of approval that *the way Jesus lived is the way God wants us all to live.* The struggle for liberation may lead to a cross, but God vindicates that way of love with an empty tomb. The world puts love to death, but God raises the dead. This is a powerful reminder for those of us joining the fight for a better world.

Every time Martin Luther King Jr. marched, held an event, or took up the cause of ending segregation, he knew he was putting his life on the line. His life was threatened countless times, and one night the situation reached an emotional climax. On January 27, 1956, King received a phone call in the middle of the night threatening to blow up his home with his wife and newborn daughter inside. He called that moment his "spiritual midnight," where he reached "the end of his powers." He wrestled with God, with fear, with exhaustion, with a loss of courage, a loss of hope, until he was suddenly struck with a deep, powerful awareness of the reality of God. King said, "I experienced the presence of the Divine as I had never experienced God before." He heard God speak. He believed God, and pressed on.

Three days later, his house was bombed, but his family was unharmed. In the aftermath of the bombing, a frightened and angry crowd of Black supporters gathered, armed and ready to find the perpetrators and exact vengeance. But from his bombed-out porch, Dr. King lifted his hand and raised his voice: "We must meet violence with nonviolence . . . We must meet hate with love. Remember, if I am stopped, this movement will not stop, because *God is with the movement.*"

This is what the cross of Jesus Christ means. In a world of hate and violence, we can have the radiant assurance that *God is with the movement.* When the kingdom of God seems to be a distant dream, when we reach our breaking point of spiritual exhaustion, the crucified and resurrected one can meet us in our spiritual midnight and remind us of a loving presence that nothing can take away from us. As Paul writes in Romans 8:35–37, "Who shall separate us from the love of Christ? Shall trouble or hardship or persecution or famine or nakedness or danger or sword? . . . No, in all these things we are more than conquerors through him who loved us."

Although Jesus's life was "stopped," the movement of the kingdom of God did not stop. Even the most brutal and degrading form of execution couldn't stop the movement of God. Jesus lives. Most Christians believe that Jesus was bodily raised in material existence. Some believe that he was raised spiritually, so that we may continue to encounter him through the divine presence. It's beyond the scope of this book to understand the mystery of the resurrection (and I suspect there is some value in remaining uncertain on the specifics), but the crucial point that all Christians basically agree on is that *Jesus now lives through us—the body of Christ.* The Spirit of Jesus lives in those who are seeking the kingdom of God, who are working for God's dream in this world.

For many conservative Christians, the resurrection is just about "proof." They believe it was the cross, not the resurrection, that accomplished salvation, because Jesus died to pay their sin-debt. The resurrection doesn't do much for them at all, except prove that Jesus is God. I don't believe the resurrection is about proof. It's not something that can be proved. We weren't there. It will never work as proof. What it gives us is *connection.* We can continue to be *connected* to Jesus and to the love of God, as we live for what Jesus lived for by the power of the Spirit.

If you are not walking out the way of Jesus toward the marginalized, then I suspect it doesn't matter if you believe something supernatural happened to Jesus's literal body; you're already disconnected from what Jesus's Spirit is doing in the world.

In this view of the cross, being "saved" doesn't mean checking a box so that you go to heaven instead of hell when you die. *Salvation is being a part of the movement of God.* It is caring about what God cares about and living for the liberation that Jesus lived—and died—for.

THE POWER OF REDEMPTIVE SUFFERING

The second thing the cross can give us is the power to reframe our suffering. It shows us how God is a master at wringing good out of evil. I want to be very careful with the idea of redemptive suffering, which has frequently been used for harm. As one of my Instagram commenters mentioned, the cross has been used as "torture porn," to glorify or even justify suffering. Throughout Christian history, people oppressed on the basis of social class, disability, gender, and more have been told that they must suffer and continue suffering, because that's just what it means to "take up their cross and follow Jesus."

There is nothing glorious about suffering. We are not meant to desire it for ourselves or others. But suffering is inevitable for all of us. And, since we can't avoid suffering, the cross does help us see how God can *redeem* it. This never justifies evil, but it keeps our hearts open and our eyes on the horizon for God to break in. We can trust that resurrection is at work, even if we don't see it. We can trust that love wins.

In a letter to his wife following the bombing of his house, Martin Luther King Jr. wrote,

> *This is the cross that we must bear for the freedom of our people. . . . I have the faith to believe that this suffering that is now coming to our family will in some little way serve to make Atlanta a better city, Georgia a better state, and America a better country. Just how I do not*

yet know, but I have faith to believe it will. . . . Our suffering is not in vain.

King had a global vision for humanity; his life was not about himself but about the whole. Richard Rohr teaches that this kind of awareness doesn't just spontaneously occur to us but often comes as a result of suffering: "The mystery of the cross has the power to teach us that our suffering is not our own and my life is not about 'me.' . . . One moves from 'me' to 'us' inside of this field of deep inner experience. This is the gateway to compassion, and thus redemption."

King said repeatedly that he did not want to be a martyr. He wanted to live. But he simultaneously held on to the hope that even if he died, all of it mattered—that, as 1 Corinthians 15:58 says, none of our labors are in vain. This faith was based on the cross. If God could turn around a gruesome execution for the redemption of the world, God could wring good out of the darkest evil.

Please hear me when I say that this is a personal journey. No one can redeem your suffering for you. Your pastor cannot tell you how you are meant to take up your cross and follow Jesus—they'll likely end up inserting their own agendas. When someone else is telling you that you must suffer for Jesus, beware! They may be using the gospel as a tool for manipulation, to keep you in line.

But when you're able to see *for yourself* how God is at work in the darkest parts of your life, just as God was at work in the cross, you will be able to access incredible courage and compassion. You will be able to say, like King, that you may not be sure how God is going to do it, but you're sure that God is alive in you. The Christian call to "die with Christ" is never the death of our *true* selves. It is the death of our fears, the death of our prejudices. The death of the shame that holds us back from the deepest love. When we follow in the way of Jesus, our true selves will be as alive as the risen Christ.

In this view of the cross, to be "saved" by the power of the death and resurrection of Jesus means putting our lives in God's hands and trusting that "this light momentary affliction is preparing for us an eternal weight of glory beyond all comparison" (2 Corinthians 4:17, ESV), as our lives become about something much bigger than ourselves.

LOVE ALL THE WAY DOWN

If there were any doubts as to the nature of the divine, the cross is meant to settle those doubts. It shows us what God is really like: God is love, all the way down.

Christians believe that the character of God is definitively revealed in the person of Jesus Christ. Jesus is the "image of the invisible God" (Colossians 1:15). Christians can argue about exactly what that means; I prefer to keep the mystery and ambiguity of the New Testament. I like how Marcus Borg explains it:

> *Jesus is, for us Christians, the decisive revelation of what a life full of God looks like. Radically centered in God and filled with the Spirit, he is the decisive disclosure and epiphany of what can be seen of God embodied in a human life. As the Word and Wisdom and Spirit of God become flesh, his life incarnates the character of God. . . . In him we see God's passion.*

Christians can see Jesus as a complete picture of what God is like, without saying that Jesus is the only way to know what God is like. We do not need to denigrate the insights of other religions to meet God in the story of Jesus. Regardless of the specific theological formulations, Christians should agree that Jesus shows us what God is like, and the cross confirms that God is defined by extravagant, unconditional love.

Our encounter with this revelation of love is meant to transform us, so that we can imitate this love in the world. In one of his most central teachings, Jesus told his disciples, "You have heard that it was said, 'You shall love your neighbor and hate your enemy.' But I say to you: Love your enemies and pray for those who persecute you, so that you may be children of your Father in heaven" (Matthew 5:43–45, NRSV). Jesus says that when we love our enemies, we are living out the reality that we are all children of God. We are all connected to each other in one global family, and when we show love for our enemies, it is an act of faith in the original goodness and divinity present in all of God's creatures. Even our worst enemies are made in God's image, and are not, in King's words, "beyond the reach of God's redemptive love."

Jesus lived this love wholeheartedly, loving his enemies all the way to death on a cross. If Jesus is the revelation of God, then the cross reveals a God who would rather die for Her enemies than punish them.

King believed that "enemy love" had the power to transform individuals, and the world. He preached, "Love is the only force capable of transforming an enemy into a friend." Love is transformational. The way that God transforms us is by loving us.

After King's house was bombed, he pleaded with his supporters not to retaliate. He knew that the only way to create a new kind of world was to break the cycles of revenge with enemy love: "While abhorring segregation, we shall love the segregationist. This is the only way to create the beloved community." The beloved community, like what Jesus called the kingdom of God, has a place for everyone at the table. While there is no room for oppression or exclusion in the kingdom of God, there is always room to forgive those who have oppressed and excluded.

Enemy love requires extreme levels of empathy. One of King's favorite phrases of Jesus was when he said during his crucifixion, "Father, forgive them, for they know not what they do" (Luke 23:34, ESV). When Jesus said this, he was talking about the Roman soldiers, who, on a literal level, knew *exactly* what they were doing. Roman soldiers had perfected the art of crucifixion. They had done it before, and they would do it again. But Jesus saw that on another level, they had no idea what they were doing. They were spiritually ignorant. They were trapped in a system of domination. They were the oppressors in that system, but they were no freer than those they oppressed. Although they held a relatively privileged position, they were also victims of the system. Jesus extends love and forgiveness to both the victims and the perpetrators. We are not free until we are all free.

This view of the cross leaves no room for an eternal hell. God's love "bears all things, believes all things, hopes all things, endures all things" (1 Corinthians 13:7, NRSV). If we didn't know this before, looking at the God of the cross, now we know. God's love isn't giving up on *anybody*.

For many of us who have deconstructed and moved away from our previous constricting religious environments, it is easy and tempting to look on everyone who hasn't left yet as hopelessly problematic. We forget that not too long ago, we were in the same system. We must hope for the redemption of everyone who takes part in the systems of oppression we experienced, even as we also work toward the destruction of those systems. Harboring bitterness against our former religious leaders is understandable, but it is a dead end that leaves us in a state of joyless disconnection. I'm not suggesting that everyone needs to be best friends with the people who hurt them, or that forgiveness should come quickly or easily. But I do believe that a truer and deeper freedom comes when we are able to love our enemies.

As the saying goes, hurt people hurt people. We have been punished, and we naturally want to punish others. Salvation is the breaking of this cycle. It lets us step out of the cycles of vengeance and become wounded healers instead of wounded punishers. The cross can do this for us.

We must be cautious with this teaching. I would never want to encourage someone to stay in a situation where they are experiencing abuse or harm out of a desire to "love their enemy." That's not what loving your enemies means. In order to love our enemies, we must first love ourselves and be utterly convinced of God's unending love for us. When we consent to our own abuse because of shame or because we believe that we deserve to suffer due to our unworthiness, we are not living in the reality of our belovedness. Loving an enemy can look like walking away from a marriage. It can look like disclosing what an abuser did. It can look like leaving a church. The difference is that when we seek justice, we are hoping for ultimate restoration, not longing for punishment.

In this view of the cross, to be "saved" means to be transformed by a vision of God's self-giving love for all people, even perpetrators, so that we can love like God loves.

SOLIDARITY WITH THE SCAPEGOATS OF HISTORY

The fourth, and possibly most powerful and subversive thing that the cross does for us, is show us *who God is with*. The

Christian doctrine of the incarnation teaches that Jesus is *Emmanuel*, which means "God is with us" in Hebrew. The cross tells us that God's "with-ness" will go to the lowest places our inhumanity takes us. In his powerful book *The Crucified God*, Jürgen Moltmann writes, "There is no loneliness and no rejection which [God] has not taken to himself and assumed in the cross. There is no cry of the oppressed which he has not heard, and no pain which he has not felt."

At the time of Jesus, the cross was not a religious symbol—it was a symbol of a shameful death for the people on the underside of history. I believe the most vivid modern allegory of the cross is the lynching tree of the white supremacist American South. Theologian James Cone draws this parallel in his masterwork *The Cross and the Lynching Tree*:

> Both the cross and the lynching tree were symbols of terror, instruments of torture and execution, reserved primarily for slaves, criminals, and insurrectionists— the lowest of the low in society. Both Jesus and blacks were publicly humiliated, subjected to the utmost indignity and cruelty. . . . In both cases, the purpose was to strike terror in the subject community. It was to let people know that the same thing would happen to them if they did not stay in their place.

The similarity between Jesus's crucifixion and lynching did not go unnoticed by Black artists and thinkers of the time, although white theologians didn't tend to make the connection. *The Crisis*, the magazine of the NAACP, edited by W. E. B. Du Bois, published a striking etching called *Christmas in Georgia: A.D. 1916* in the December 1916 issue. The haunting piece depicts a Black man being lynched by a white mob, while Jesus Christ surrounds and upholds him. In a speech bubble, Christ's words read: "Inasmuch as ye did it unto the least of these, My brethren, ye did it unto Me."

It must not be ignored that the white mobs who hoisted innocent Black bodies for ritual murder were made up of Christians. They worshiped a white Christ and sang songs looking forward to their eternal salvation in heaven, all while they recrucified Christ on earth, over and over again. But as Cone writes, "If the God of Jesus' cross is found among the least, the crucified people of the world, then God is also found among those lynched in American history." The message of the cross is that God is not on the side of the powerful, whether they are Christians or not. God is on the side of the suffering. God is with the scapegoats.

One of the tragic facts of civilization is the way groups of people create enemies that do not exist. The philosopher and anthropologist René Girard calls this the *scapegoat mechanism*. Majority groups choose a marginalized group and blame them for all problems, real and imaginary, leading to exclusion and violence against the marginalized. The Nazis made the Jews the scapegoat for their social ills. Southern whites did it to Black people. We see the scapegoat mechanism today in the way many conservatives talk about immigrants crossing the southern border, supposedly coming to take their jobs. This tribal mindset creates cohesion and identity for the in-group, as they unite around their shared enemy. This happens over and over throughout history. We create enemies that do not exist, and we pour out our violence and hatred on them. We crucify them.

On the cross, Jesus joins the scapegoats of history and unmasks the injustice and brutality of our human systems of power and exclusion. When Jesus calls us to take up our crosses, he is inviting us to join him on the margins and stand with those who are at risk of being destroyed by the systems of domination we create. This will often be costly. Father Gregory Boyle says, "Jesus just stood with the outcasts until they were welcomed or until he was crucified—whichever came first."

The cross shows us what the kingdoms of this world do. They scapegoat and crucify people, especially people on the margins and those who stand with people on the margins, like Jesus. But the resurrection tells us what God does. God sides with the suffering of marginalized people and the victims of history, and works to bring life out of death.

The queer therapist Matthias Roberts, who grew up a conservative evangelical, saw this scapegoat mechanism at play in the way his church community excluded queer people and blamed the LGBTQ community for the social problems in America. The Bible really says very little about gay people (actually nothing at all, when you consider that its authors were not aware of the concept of queerness as a sexual orientation the way we are). And yet queer people receive a disproportionate amount of hateful attention from conservative Christians. This is scapegoating.

Roberts was denied his humanity as a queer person within evangelicalism, but he saw in the gospel that Jesus was on the side of the scapegoats, not on the side of the power structures. Jesus was with him in his queerness, not with the church that excluded him! Roberts came to see the cross and resurrection as a hopeful message that God is working on behalf of the victims of history. One piece of evidence for this that Roberts points out is that "victims and scapegoats are being listened to more now than ever before in all human history." This is good news. This is the power of the resurrection.

In 2024, Easter happened to fall on March 31, the International Transgender Day of Visibility. This made a lot of

Christians very upset; they complained that their celebration of Jesus was being replaced with a "nefarious LGBTQ agenda." But as I reflect on the meaning of the cross, I believe seeing and celebrating trans people is completely in line with the message of Easter. The fact that the international community recognizes a day to see and listen to trans people is evidence of the arc of history moving toward justice. The Spirit of the living Christ is at work! But this struggle is far from over.

Right now, our beloved trans siblings are being scapegoated around the world. They are being crucified. In the United States, trans people are two and a half times more likely to experience violence than cisgender people. Worse, the number of trans people murdered in the United States has doubled over the last few years, with a disproportionate number of victims being Black trans women. And instead of responding to this wave of violence and terror with compassion, our country is doubling down on anti-trans hate. In 2024, there were 669 bills across forty-three states being pushed to block the rights of trans people to publicly exist.

If you think that the cross and resurrection are mostly about keeping people out of hell in the next world, then you'll miss how crosses are still going up in this world, especially for marginalized people. I am absolutely convinced that if Jesus were walking the earth today, he would draw especially near to the trans community, showing them love, acceptance, and solidarity. He would have gone to every length. He would have gone to the cross fighting for them. Now, as the body of Christ, that's what *we* are supposed to do.

In this view of the cross, to be "saved" means to stand in solidarity with the same people as Jesus. We put a stop to scapegoating by joining Jesus among the marginalized. In that place, we experience the power of the resurrection.

SAVED BY THE POWER OF THE CROSS

So, did Jesus "die for our sin"? Yes, I believe he did. But not for the individual sins that you and I commit, the little ledger of our wrongdoings. Jesus wasn't crucified because you touched yourself.

Jesus was an innocent victim, a loving person living in connection with God, himself, and others, and yet he was thrown into the Valley of Slaughter. Like countless other victims throughout history, Jesus endured hell on earth. Hell—Gehenna—is a place of weeping, torment, and death. It is the natural consequence of our superiority, exclusion, and violence toward others and ourselves.

On the cross, Jesus went through hell—not in the sense that he was punished in our place so that God isn't forced to punish us, but in the sense that *Jesus did not sow the seeds of hell, but he reaped hell anyway.* He reaped the violence that other people sowed. That's how he died for our sin. His life of love reveals where our hateful actions lead, and when we see this, and when we are moved by it, we have the opportunity to be transformed by this vision of love and called to a better way. We can be saved.

In this chapter, we have looked at many ways that the cross can contribute to a spirituality of love, with no need for hell or a punishing God. I still believe in the power of the cross, but not because I think Jesus died for my sins so that I can avoid eternal punishment.

The cross shows me what God wants: liberation. The cross reminds me that God is with the movement of the kingdom of God, and that wherever we struggle for justice against the forces of domination, God is with us, even when the odds are against us.

The cross shows me what God can do: God can redeem even the darkest sorrows. A vision of the cross can give me hope that God is at work in my suffering. God is not the author of evil, but God can wring good out of bad.

The cross shows me what God is like: love, all the way down. A never-stopping love, for the victims and the perpetrators. This is a God who would rather suffer for their enemies than punish them.

The cross shows me who God is with: the marginalized, the scapegoats of history, the suffering ones. And God invites me to join Jesus there.

Ultimately, if you have been wounded by the way Christians have brutalized the message of the cross, I do not want to pressure you to reclaim something that has hurt you. But many have found a spiritual pathway through the cross into deeper connection with the love of God. The good news is, God's presence with you and love for you are not dependent on what you believe about the cross. The cross itself shows us that you couldn't break free from God's love if you tried.

11.

GOING THROUGH HELL

*If There's No Hell, What Does It Mean
to Be Born Again?*

The dark night of the soul comes just before revelation.
The cave you fear to enter holds the treasure you seek.

—Joseph Campbell

In evangelicalism and many other forms of Christianity, "getting saved" or "being born again" is primarily a transaction to make sure we go to heaven instead of hell. You say a prayer to accept Jesus into your heart by putting your faith in his finished work on the cross, and then your sins are placed on Jesus's account, so that God can forgive you and accept you. It may have implications for this life, but it is primarily about the next life. This raises a question: If we reject this idea—if we believe that God is not going to punish us, and there is no torment waiting for us in the afterlife to avoid, and the cross was not about a cosmic transaction with God— then what does it mean to be born again? Do we actually need to be saved? In this chapter, we will explore some of the Christian images of salvation and what they can still teach us about our journeys of spiritual transformation.

Many of us would be perfectly fine to leave the idea of being born again in the trash bin, since it is so deeply associated with coercive, even abusive, fundamentalism. If that's you, by all means, feel free to jettison this language. But as with the cross, I believe there is a powerful symbolism here that we can reclaim and use for good. When we understand rebirth as a metaphor for transformation, we can see this mythical pattern at work in our spirituality, drawing us deeper into union with God, ourselves, and others. In other parts of this book, I have talked about salvation in terms of social justice. I do believe that there is a social and political aspect to salvation that is often ignored in evangelicalism. Jesus doesn't just save individual souls; Jesus wants to save the world! But the spirituality of Jesus also has a powerful picture of personal salvation—it's just not about being saved from hell. It's about being saved from a life of disconnection and self-obsession. It's about being saved *for love*.

Jesus uses phrases like *born again* and *born of the Spirit* to describe spiritual rebirth in John 3, but this concept of inner transformation is even more commonly described in the New Testament with the image of *dying and rising*. Our spiritual journey away from ego and disconnection, into connection and union with God, can be mapped onto Jesus's journey of death and resurrection.

Like so many aspects of doctrine, the details of this journey are a matter of debate among Christians. Jesus died on the cross and was resurrected three days later, but what happened in between? One common belief, reflected in the Apostles' Creed, is that while Jesus was dead, he descended into hell as a conqueror, liberating those who were imprisoned by death because they had died earlier in history.

The harrowing of hell, as this idea is known, was a celebrated doctrine for the first few centuries of the church, and one of the most commonly painted scenes in religious art. In many Eastern Orthodox churches today, you will still find images of Jesus entering hell and leading out a train of captives, in a kind of transcendental prison break. Evangelicals, however, rarely discuss this doctrine, because it implies that salvation is something that can happen after death, which defies their core assumptions about salvation. If Jesus could deliver souls from hell once, then why couldn't the love of God continue to liberate souls after death, eventually drawing all people into the love of God? To empty hell one time in history and then let it fill right back up again for eternity seems incoherent.

I am quite agnostic on the literalness of Jesus's descent into hell—but I am a passionate believer in the spiritual, mythical reality of it. Joseph Campbell famously said that "mythology is not a lie. . . . Mythology is the penultimate truth—penultimate because the ultimate cannot be put into words. It is beyond words."

Remember, as a metaphor, hell is absolutely real. We all go through it. Going through hell is not about punishment; it is the disconnection and sense of separation that is baked into the human experience. But it is also a necessary waypoint on our path toward resurrection, just like it was for Jesus. With the harrowing of hell, Jesus shows us that the journey into wholeness and spiritual transformation goes down before it goes up. As Ephesians 4:10 (ESV) says, "He who descended is the one who also ascended far above all the heavens, that he might fill all things."

Over the last few years, I have gone through my own personal hell. First, in my process of deconstruction, I stepped down from my role as a pastor, a job I once thought I would do for the rest of my life. I not only lost my church community, I lost my identity, all while reconsidering some of my core beliefs. If I wasn't a pastor, who was I? If I was no longer a part of the evangelical community, who were my people? Who had my back? I started taking anxiety medication for the first time. I found solace in my family, and in knowing that my wife was on a similar trajectory of deconstruction. I leaned on her a lot.

But then, a little over a year after I left the ministry, my wife asked me for a separation. It was difficult for me to hear or understand where she was coming from, because it splintered the last remaining solid piece of my world. I was no longer a pastor. Now, I would no longer be a husband. She has her own story, and her own journey of discovering herself on the other side of evangelicalism that isn't mine to share. I will simply say that she saw what many of us have come to see: that so many of her major life decisions were driven by compliance to the evangelical road map for her life and submission to spiritual (patriarchal) authorities, all undergirded by the fear of hell. She was asking herself what she really wanted in life for the first time. It was startling for me to realize that I was not a part of that for her. My world was turned upside down.

The year that followed was a year of suffering, tears, revelation, and transformation. When I moved out of our family house into a rented duplex, I was not only an emotional wreck, I was also embarrassed. No surprise: People have *opinions* about pastors getting divorced. I had to die to whatever sense of respectability I was clinging to. Die to what people thought I was supposed to be. Die to what *I* thought I was supposed to be.

I learned more about myself then than during any other time of my life. I got more honest with myself and other people than I had ever been. I rescued a sweet pit bull named Maev and went on a lot of walks. I started dating outside of purity culture for the first time, with the help of a sex therapist. I grieved my mistakes and losses, and began to embrace reality. I decorated the hell out of that duplex, covering the walls with art and album covers, making it a home for me and my kids. Feeling I had nothing more to lose, I became the most authentic and vulnerable version of myself. I felt born again. And it turns out that experience is a spiritual pattern found in almost every ancient religion, and it is especially exemplified for Christians by Jesus Christ. Death leads to resurrection. Before Jesus ascends as the risen Christ, he descends into hell.

Many of you reading this book have walked through your own version of hell. That's often what it takes to start rethinking your whole spirituality. If you have begun to deconstruct your faith, you know how painful that can be. You may have had to walk away from a religious community. You may have endured rejection from friends or family. You may have been condemned by church leaders. You may have had to sort through the various ways you were indoctrinated, trying to make peace with how your life was shaped by harmful and exclusionary beliefs. Working through all of that is gutting. It is hell. It can feel like you're losing your identity. It can feel like you're coming apart.

The good news is that inside that fiery furnace, which can feel like dying, you have the opportunity to become the most alive and whole version of yourself. That's the pattern of spirituality we follow in Jesus Christ. Jesus doesn't save us *from* hell; he saves us right through it.

DYING WITH CHRIST

I have a lot of tattoos—thirty-seven at the time of writing, possibly more by the time you're reading this (who can say how the Spirit will lead?). But of all those pieces, only one is a Bible verse. Surprising for a tatted pastor, I know, but too many can get corny. I chose this verse because I felt it summarized the Christian message, and although I interpret it differently than I used to, I still believe that. Here's the verse; the reference is inked on a dagger going through my collarbone.

> *I have been crucified with Christ. It is no longer I who*
> *live, but Christ who lives in me. And the life I now live*

*in the flesh I live by faith in the Son of God, who loved
me and gave himself for me.*

Galatians 2:20, ESV

With these words, Paul says that for him to follow Christ
meant following him into crucifixion. Something had to die.
When he says, "It is no longer I who live," we may think he
means that he has lost himself. But when Paul says *Christ*
lives in him, he does not mean that his identity is lost in Jesus's identity. Christ is not Jesus's last name; *Christ* means
"the anointed." Christ is the divine that inhabits material existence. Christ lives in us, because we bear the image of God;
we are "partakers of the divine nature" (2 Peter 1:4, ESV).

The spiritual mystics tell us that we all have "false selves,"
which are culturally constructed.* Some have called this the
ego. The ego constructs identities to gain belovedness. Remember what clinical psychologist Dr. Becky Kennedy says:
"In our early years, our body is learning under what conditions we receive love and attention and understanding and
affection, and under what conditions we get rejected, punished, and left alone." Like Adam and Eve, we learn to cover
our shame with the fig leaves of the false self. We do this because we forget the inherent belovedness of our true self. We
identify ourselves with things like political parties, sports
teams, relationship statuses, ethnic groups, material possessions, and, yes, even religious beliefs, in order to construct
our identities. But these things are not *who we really are.* They
are superficial selves that cause us to feel superior to others
and therefore disconnect us from others.

---

* See Thomas Merton, *New Seeds of Contemplation* (New York: New Directions, 1961) for a powerful treatment of this subject.

My truest self is the part of me that is connected to God. We are all made from love and inhabited by God, and therefore we are all already connected to each other, and we are already perfectly loved by God. Our constructed identities and our bids for love do not make us any more beloved. God is in me, and I am safe in God's love. This is always true, but I'm not always aware of it. I am often living in a delusion of separateness and superiority, fueled by the insecurity of the false self. This is what needs to die so that God's life can live in me.

This is why Jesus says that when we lose our life following him, we will find it. Paul says that when we *die* with Christ, we *live* by faith in Christ who loves us. The more we die, the more we love. We go through hell so that we can come out on the other side more faithful, more loving, more connected to the divine presence inside us and inside all creation.

Unfortunately, this teaching has been misinterpreted and abused. Many of us who were raised in evangelicalism were told we are supposed to "die to ourselves," and in the process, we lost ourselves. We didn't learn how to listen to ourselves or protect ourselves. Women were often told that they needed to die to themselves in their marriages and serve their husbands. Queer people were told they needed to die to themselves and reject their identities for the sake of the kingdom of God. I was told that the secret to joy was JOY: Jesus first, Others second, and Yourself last. I don't believe that's what dying and rising with Christ is about.

We put our false selves to death so that our true selves can come to life. "Christ in you" is not a separate person from you. It is the best and truest part of yourself. If Jesus ever calls us to "come and die," he also calls us to "come forth" from our tombs, *more deeply ourselves than ever before.*

Every death is a resurrection. This is the pattern. Hell is never the end. It is as Jesus taught, "unless a grain of wheat falls into the earth and dies, it remains alone; but if it dies, it bears much fruit" (John 12:24, ESV).

RISING WITH CHRIST

When my wife and I separated, it took a while for the realization to settle in that things were never going back to the way they were. This was a hard pill to swallow. We have three young boys and an adult daughter. I love parenting, but never in my life did I picture myself as a single dad. Three wild boys can be overwhelming. Before, when I got dysregulated, I could "tap out" and take a break, let my wife step in while I took some breaths. Now, all of a sudden, there was no other person. There was no stepping away. When I parent now, it's just me. This was quite the adjustment at first. I've gotten so much better at solo parenting over the last several years, but I still have very difficult days where it feels impossible.

One time, I lost my temper on the way to church. My three boys decided that buckling their seat belts was negotiable and refused to comply with the commands I shouted into the back seat with increasing frustration while driving on the highway. That car drive felt like hell to me.

When we walked into church, late and frazzled, the congregation was already singing: "Christ is risen from the dead, trampling over death by death."

"If Christ is risen," I thought, "why does my entire life feel like it's been nailed shut in a coffin and buried in the dirt?" I did not feel risen. I felt defeated. I texted a friend, "I wanna quit." I didn't mean I wanted to quit my life altogether. Parents know the kind of quit I meant; I wanted to quit that car drive, climb under the covers, hand them all iPads, and not be responsible for anyone for a while. But I had to keep going.

And later that day, when we got home from church, after I cried a little, and cursed a little, I had several moments that reminded me of resurrection. I threw a football with my seven-year-old and played a game where we each did a little spin move every time we caught the ball. My nine-year-old slept in bed with me, something he never used to do when I was married and probably won't do many more times. I savored it.

My identities of "pastor" and "husband" died a painful death, but my true self did not die. Reckoning with those losses has caused me to wake up to the connections that matter most. In many ways, my relationship with each of my kids has been better, stronger, and more intentional since my separation. In fact, because of these pains and losses, I love more deeply in every area of my life. This is the fruit. This is how you know you are on the path of dying and rising with Christ: you are growing in love. In fact, I now believe that growing in love is the only salvation worth caring about. We are saved for love.

There are days when, if I could, I would change it all. I would rewrite my history, remove the downward slumps. Erase the divorce, the deconstruction, the mistakes, the failures. I'm sure you know what I mean. But if I erased those moments, I would erase myself. I am able to love like I love because of those moments.

It's probably why Richard Rohr says that after the age of thirty, success has nothing more to teach us. It feels nice, but it doesn't unlock new levels of growth. By the second half of life, all of our growth will come from "failure, humiliation, and suffering; things falling apart. Dissolution is the only thing that allows the soul to go to a deeper place."

Jonah prayed from the whale's belly, "Out of the belly of

hell cried I, and Thou heardest my voice" (Jonah 2:2, KJV). When we fall into the belly of hell, it is an opportunity to wake up from our delusion of separation and become aware of our connectedness. Borg writes, "We are all already in relationship to God and have been from our birth . . . spirituality is about becoming aware of a relationship that already exists." Waking up to this reality—to the reality of our belovedness—is what it means to be saved. This is not a one-time thing. I've been in the belly of hell before, and I will be there again. I will keep dying, and by God's grace, I will keep rising. I will be born again, and again, and again.

So do we *need* to be saved? It depends what you mean by "need." We certainly don't need it to avoid punishment. We need salvation like we need love. And it is often in the belly of hell—where our false selves are stripped away—that we can discover the love that was there all along.

12.

THE OPEN TABLE

*If There's No Hell,
Do "Unbelievers" Need to
Become Christians?*

I take my cue from Jesus Christ, really, who told me and told all of us to love each other, clothe the naked, feed the hungry, and visit those in prison. If you can't do that, you're not a believer—I don't care what church you go to.

—James Baldwin

In 1966, the Buddhist monk Thich Nhat Hanh visited the United States as a part of an interfaith protest against the war in Vietnam. During this time, he met with several Christian leaders working for peace, including Martin Luther King Jr., Thomas Merton, and Daniel Berrigan.

Nhat Hanh later wrote, "The moment I met Martin Luther King, Jr., I knew I was in the presence of a holy person. . . . His very being was a source of great inspiration for me" and "made me feel that Lord Jesus is still here with us." After his encounter with these Christians, united in their joint quest for peace, Nhat Hanh added an image of Jesus to the altar in his hermitage next to the image of Buddha, symbolizing that he felt spiritual roots in both traditions.

The impact of this interfaith meeting went both ways. Merton, a Catholic priest and mystic, was deeply moved by their connection. In a staggering statement, this Catholic priest wrote that Nhat Hanh "is more my brother than many who are nearer to me by race and nationality, because he and I see things exactly the same way. He and I deplore the war that is ravaging his country. We deplore it for exactly the same reasons: human reasons, reasons of sanity, justice and love."

Most American Christians, however, did not share the sentiment. Most denominations supported the draft, which sent almost a million young American men into the horror of an immoral, ideological war, disproportionately impacting minorities and the poor. Although some progressive Christians, like King, Merton, and Berrigan, spoke out against the war, on the whole, Christians were more concerned with fighting atheistic Communism than with seeking peace.

It is easy to see why Merton believed he had more in common with Nhat Hanh than with those of his own country and religion, who did not know what made for peace. According to evangelical dogma, Nhat Hanh is going to hell. Merton's commonality with him is heresy. Merton should have been witnessing to him, not experiencing solidarity. But Merton was a mystic. He was a Christian, but he knew that God was not *owned* by Christians. God is not owned by anyone. God is a universal spirit of love and is the inheritance of all people. Merton knew that Nhat Hanh did not need to *get* saved. In their shared quest for justice and love, Merton saw that Nhat Hanh was seeking the kingdom of God; he was saved already.

This is why, although I'm a Christian, I do not believe it's essential for people to *become* Christians to experience healthy spirituality or be connected to God.

At this point, you may feel that I'm presenting a vision of Christianity that is almost unrecognizable from what you were raised with. But this isn't just based on my opinion. I believe that broad, inclusive universalism was central to the message of Jesus. As we will see, universal inclusion is quite clear in the overarching message of scripture. It's just that our fixation on hell, damnation, and being right has blinded us to it. We've been so focused on the idea that "unsaved" people were going to hell that we missed what hell actually was. We missed that our exclusivism and exclusion actually *created* hell, for ourselves and others.

Dogmatic, hell-centered Christianity fueled colonialism throughout the world, contributing to global suffering and oppression for millions of people. People who believed that they were right about God and Indigenous people were wrong violently forced their religion on the world, creating a global system of white Christian patriarchal supremacy. Christian colonialism made hell on earth.

Christian exclusivism does not just damage non-Christians; it has spiritually impoverished Christians as well. Jesus invites everyone to a banquet, and *the very nature of hell is refusing to join the party.* When we refuse to acknowledge the universal scope of grace, it keeps us in hell. It keeps us disconnected from our neighbors, both local and global. It keeps us out of the divine dance of grace.

GOOD NEWS FOR ALL NATIONS

I know thinking of the world this way is quite a dramatic shift from the versions of Christianity many of us were raised with, in which convincing other people to become Christians was so central. Many of us struggle to understand what the point of the church or the Christian life is without the need to save people from hell. If there's no hell, does becoming a Christian matter? What does *evangelism* mean? What was Jesus talking about when he gave us "the Great Commission" and told us to "go and make disciples of all nations, baptizing them in the name of the Father and of the Son and of the Holy Spirit, and teaching them to obey everything I have commanded you" (Matthew 28:19–20)?

For evangelicals, this is one of the most important passages in the whole Bible. (It makes sense that *evangelicals* would be all about *evangelism.*) But was Jesus talking about convincing everyone to convert to Christianity?

When Jesus spoke those words, there was no Christian religion, and there were no Christian institutions. There were no Christian creeds. There had not been any Christian councils. There hadn't been any heretics burned at the stake for disagreeing with doctrinal formulations or the authority of the pope. What there was, was the kingdom of God. There was the radical life and example of Jesus Christ. And his message and example actually call us away from exclusionary thinking into an inclusive vision of the kingdom, which even includes people of other religious beliefs.

While Jesus certainly loved people of his own ethnicity, he also saw that God was not confined to any single nation or ethnicity. He spoke of God as a loving Father to all creation, who "causes his sun to rise on the evil and the good, and sends rain on the righteous and the unrighteous" (Matthew 5:45). Jesus told his followers that the family of God was for every kind of person, from every kind of place. Jesus's commission to go to the nations was not a call to dominate other cultures but to lovingly engage beyond our tribalistic tendencies with the ways God is at work all around the world, in other cultures, and even in other religions.

The call to go to the nations was never supposed to justify colonialism—it was an invitation into inclusion. But it has been used for coercion and superiority. "All nations" means that *God is for everybody.* God is not owned by one people or one religion. We are all a part of this together.

This theme of God's universal love and welcome for all people runs through the entire Bible and is ever widening. When God first speaks to Abram in Genesis, the promise is that through him, "all the families of the earth shall be blessed" (Genesis 12:3, ESV). Although Yahweh is often depicted as a tribal God in the Hebrew Bible, exclusively focused on the people of Israel, the expansive hope of the prophets is that *through* Israel, God's light would "reach to the ends of the earth" (Isaiah 49:6). The promise is that God's Spirit would "pour out . . . on all people" (Joel 2:28), indicating that all people have access to connection with God through God's universal Spirit.

Jesus was always seeking to fulfill this universal vision. The Gospel of Matthew shows us that universal inclusion is at the heart of Jesus's identity by including the Magi (or, as we often call them, the three wise men) in his birth narrative. They were likely Zoroastrian astrologers and as such would have been considered pagans by Jews at the time and by most Christians today. And yet they are depicted as genuine seekers of truth. They were drawn by God's Spirit to the Christ child. They do not convert to Judaism or Christianity, and yet their worship is received and celebrated by God. God's real presence in their lives is acknowledged. This is almost certainly a mythical story, not a historical one, but Matthew includes it because this universal welcome is at the heart of the purpose of Jesus.

Jesus illustrates this multiple times in his ministry. In the parable of the good Samaritan, we learn that one's loving actions toward others matter far more than religious affiliation. As I've mentioned, Jesus's community saw Samaritans as despised heretics, so the phrase *good Samaritan* was an oxymoron to them. Yet the foreign, "unbelieving" Samaritan is the one who exemplifies the kingdom of God, while those with "good doctrine" pass by the wounded man on a road to Gehenna. If the good Samaritan visited an evangelical church, he wouldn't even be permitted to take Communion. But in Jesus's story, the heretical Samaritan is not only "saved," he is the bringer of salvation. The "other" becomes the savior.

Jesus knows that salvation often comes where we least expect it, in the form of the one we are most likely to exclude. I'm not using the word *salvation* to talk about our afterlife destination—I'm talking about the state of our souls in *this life*. Our exclusivism damns us, not to hell but to a state of separation from our brothers and sisters. We are saved when we let go of our superiority and our need to exclude, when we see that our savior is present in "the least of these."

Jesus makes this inclusion explicit when he heals the servant of a Roman centurion. Centurions weren't just any soldiers; they held a prestigious and well-paying rank in the Roman military. This centurion seeks out Jesus for help and healing, despite the way he would have been socialized to think of a foreign peasant like Jesus as entirely beneath him. The Roman centurion was a cultural elite from the most powerful civilization in the world. Jesus was a homeless prophet in a territory being occupied and ruled by that civilization. To get an idea of the dynamic, imagine a white, Christian Marine Corps colonel coming to an Islamic sage with no political power in Afghanistan and asking him for spiritual direction—it might be a great idea, but it's almost impossible to imagine it actually happening.

What stands in the way of this? A sense of cultural and religious superiority. Ethnocentrism. Racism. Classism. When the centurion asked Jesus for help, he defied those oppressive forces. Jesus is "amazed" by the centurion's faith (Matthew 8:10). He doesn't encourage him to turn away from Roman paganism or convert to Judaism or Christianity. In fact, Jesus sees his faith as a paradigm of what he is trying to do in his ministry and says to his disciples, "Truly I tell you, I have not found anyone in Israel with such great faith. I say to you that many will come from the east and the west, and will take their places at the feast with Abraham, Isaac and Jacob in the kingdom of heaven. But the subjects of the kingdom will be thrown outside, into the darkness, where there will be weeping and gnashing of teeth" (Matthew 8:10–12).

Why was Jesus so impressed by the centurion's faith? It

wasn't that the Roman centurion believed that Jesus was God in the flesh, or that Jesus was going to die for his sins. This centurion had no understanding of Christian doctrines. (No one did yet.) The faith Jesus commended was the way that the centurion recognized God's Spirit was at work in Jesus, even though Jesus was far outside of his own Roman culture.

In a world of division, where we believe that *our* people and *our* culture are in the right and other people need *our* answers, this centurion believed that God was at work in a culture very different from his own. Instead of seeing Jesus as beneath him, he entered a posture of mutuality and curiosity, and because of that, he received a gift. Jesus became his savior. The centurion found his savior in the face of the cultural "other."

And Jesus sees this as a prototype of the kingdom he is building, where brothers and sisters from the east and the west join together as one global family, united by our common humanity and our shared divinity, united by the Spirit that falls on all flesh, united by love. To refuse this welcome, to exclude rather than include, to see other people and nations and cultures as lesser—Jesus tells us that is the definition of hell.

Jesus laments that the religious leaders of Jerusalem were unable to grasp this universal vision, even though they were supposed to be the light to the nations. Their nationalism and exclusivism were going to lead them to "weeping and gnashing of teeth"—to Gehenna.

Hell is what happens when we fail to recognize our connection to each other. Like the older brother in Jesus's parable of the prodigal son, our need to exclude keeps us outside pouting while inside the Father is throwing a universal party of every tribe, tongue, and nation.

When Jesus overturned the profiteering in the Temple courtyard, he quoted the prophet Jeremiah: "Is it not written: 'My house will be called a house of prayer for *all nations*'?" (Mark 11:17, emphasis mine). Biblical scholar Marcus Borg writes that for Jesus, the Temple "was universal. It was not to be the private possession of a particular group, not even of the holy people." Jesus believed that for the Temple to reflect God's heart, it must be a place where we come to recognize that we are all God's children, and the things that divide us are imaginary and insignificant compared to the Spirit that connects us.

EVERYONE IS CLEAN

After Jesus's time on earth, when the church started to try to live out his vision of the kingdom of God, they immediately ran into questions of how to include outsiders. In fact, arguably the most central question that the early church wrestles with in the letters that make up the New Testament is whether Gentiles needed to convert to Judaism in order to be accepted by God.

You have to remember that Christianity as a religion did not exist in the lifetimes of Jesus or the apostle Paul (who wrote most of those New Testament letters). They were Jewish, and they believed Jesus to be the fulfillment of their Jewish faith. However, they were immediately confronted with the universalism of Jesus's message. When Gentiles began following the way of Jesus, they faced a debate over whether they needed to be circumcised or eat kosher in accordance with Jewish religious laws. When the early church eventually chose to set aside these requirements, they were setting aside dozens of Bible verses and clear commands in scripture, because they decided that *loving and including people mattered more than following the Bible.* Or, really, it would be more accurate to say they knew that in the end they *were* following the Bible, because the ultimate fulfillment of all biblical commands is love.

Religious Jews had devoutly practiced circumcision for centuries, so it's hard to overstate how shocking it would have been when Paul wrote, "For in Christ Jesus neither circumcision nor uncircumcision has any value." But in the next sentence, he explains why: "The only thing that counts is faith expressing itself through love" (Galatians 5:6). I do not believe Paul meant that we were supposed to replace the old ritual of circumcision with a new exclusionary ritual like baptism or the Eucharist in order to be in a relationship with God. Any of these rituals can be meaningful and special, but their purpose is not to grant certain people a connection to God while keeping others out. Paul's point is that our national or religious backgrounds make no difference when it comes to our connection to God. There can be no more gatekeeping. Everybody can get in on this.

Peter makes a similar point about dietary laws. In Acts 10, he receives a vision in which God explicitly tells him to eat nonkosher animals. Again, it is difficult for us to comprehend how central these dietary restrictions were to Peter's religious identity. Setting them aside meant setting aside dozens and dozens of Bible verses. Understandably, Peter initially objects, saying, "Surely not, Lord! . . . I have never eaten anything impure or unclean" (Acts 10:14). But God responds, "Do not call anything impure that God has made clean" (Acts 10:15).

As soon as this vision is over, Peter receives word that a Roman centurion wants to meet with him, having had a vision of his own. Peter understands the vision wasn't just about food—it was about who gets a seat at God's table. God was talking about people. So he goes and meets with the centurion and the "large gathering of people" he has with him, telling them, "God has shown me that I should not call anyone impure or unclean" (Acts 10:27–28). Man-made religious rules are always putting limits on love, but to God, no one is impure. Everyone is clean.

Take a moment and breathe in this truth. It's stated so clearly in our Bible, and yet many of us received the *exact opposite message*. I was told that I was born unclean. I was told that gay people were impure. I was told that Muslims and Buddhists and Catholics were unsaved. This was the message of evangelicalism—but this was not the message of Jesus.

Peter summarizes his profound realization:

> *I now realize how true it is that God does not show favoritism but accepts from every nation the one who fears him and does what is right. You know the message God sent to the people of Israel, announcing the good news of peace through Jesus Christ, who is Lord of all.*

Acts 10:34–36

We show favoritism, but God does not. God accepts everyone. God cares about how we treat one another, but God is not auditing our beliefs. The good news—the gospel of Jesus—is a message of peace and reconciliation.

Peter says that Jesus is Lord of all. That is not an exclusive message. It is the very inclusivity of Jesus Christ that makes him Lord of *all*! Lords of this world demand allegiances that divide us. Religious nationalism causes us to center *our* people over *all* people. Coming under the Lordship of Jesus, on the other hand, must mean making reconciliation and universal acceptance more central than our national or religious identities.

Jesus the welcoming one is Lord of *all*, and that means all are accepted. All are loved. Just as they are. And no, you do not need to explicitly call Jesus Lord in order to recognize and embody this truth.

Now, there are a handful of passages that may seem exclusionary at first glance. The one I am asked about most frequently is John 14:6, where Jesus says, "I am the way and the truth and the life. No one comes to the Father except through me." Thich Nhat Hanh, as a Buddhist, is not bothered by this supposedly exclusionary verse. He writes,

> *When Jesus said "I am the way," he meant that to have a true relationship with God, you must practice his way. . . . His life, which is the way. If you do not really look at his life, you cannot see the way. If you only satisfy yourself with praising a name, even the name of Jesus, it is not practicing the life of Jesus. We must practice living deeply, loving, and acting with charity if we truly wish to honor Jesus.*

Ironically, when Christians use a handful of verses to build dogmatic systems of exclusion around Jesus, they are actually moving further from *the way* of Jesus. In their insistence that everyone praise the name of Jesus, they are not practicing the life of Jesus.

When I think about how I used to view people of other faiths, I weep. I am weeping now, mourning the years I lost while fearfully judging instead of curiously listening. With a closed heart, I believed that some people were impure and unclean. Jesus came to show us just the opposite. Jesus's message was the declaration that God is not for *some* people, but for *all* people. This is the good news. This is the gospel. When we miss this, we miss out on the gifts we can receive from others who differ from us.

White evangelical spirituality has a tendency toward cultural superiority. Growing up, I was taught that tarot cards were evil, yoga poses were demon worship, and Eastern meditation practices were dangerous. At fundamentalist summer camp, we were taught that rock and roll was inherently evil because the syncopated rhythms came from African tribal music, which had demonic roots. Anything that didn't come from a white, European, Christian cultural background was dismissed as not merely irrelevant but actually *satanic*.

But think about it: The Magi who visited Jesus used astrology, which many Christians regard as pagan, and yet it led them to Christ! The gifts they gave to Jesus were not rejected as the fruits of a pagan culture; they were received as evidence of the universal reach of God's love. When we let go of our exclusivism, we are free to enjoy the gifts that come from other traditions. We are free to see how much we can learn from each other.

This white Christian supremacist perspective on other cultures and religions has impoverished our tradition, making it unable to learn from the best of other traditions. No tradition has a monopoly on truth, and we have so much to learn from the great spiritual practices of the world. We can revel in the poetry of Rumi, the Islamic mystic. We can learn from the Hindu concept of Brahman, the ultimate reality and source of all being, which can be a helpful way to think about God. We can also learn from the various branches of the Christian church, such as the Eastern Orthodox tradition, which does not teach original sin and instead emphasizes our inner divinity.

I am not suggesting that all religions are the same. They often view God and the world very differently. But those differences do not make other religions evil or worthless, and they do not mean that the Spirit of God cannot be touched from within any religion.

I have personally found Buddhist mindfulness exercises to be incredibly helpful in my spirituality. Mindful breathing brings me back into my body. Embodiment is not typically emphasized in Christianity, but it has been an important practice for me to connect to my own inner light. This is a gift from another tradition that has enriched me.

Many of my friends have found incredible spiritual value in reconnecting with their ancestral religious practices. For example, my friend Keri has rediscovered the spiritual value of her Indigenous roots. Christian colonialism painted Indigenous practices as pagan, but she has found wisdom and beauty there that strengthens her relationship to the Spirit of Christ. Similarly, many Black Christians have found spiritual power in incorporating traditional African understandings of ancestors into their spirituality. Rituals of remembrance of ancestors are an act of defiance against the colonizing mindset, which worked to wipe out African identity. As D. Danyelle Thomas powerfully reminds us, "For Black folks (and, I imagine, other people of the global majority), convincing us to recognize our inherited spiritual practices as demonic is the greatest trick white supremacy has ever pulled on us." Reclaiming these practices reminds Indigenous and Black people that their roots are not demonic. It was the violence of colonial white supremacy that was truly demonic. Their cultural background is "very good" (Genesis 1:31) and beloved by God.

A dogmatic spirituality of fear and punishment makes it impossible to receive these gifts and see where the Spirit is already at work in other traditions. Our sense of superiority cuts us off from the richness of being a part of one global family with many spiritual brothers and sisters.

WHAT IS OUR MISSION?

I know this can be a seismic shift for those of us who were raised in evangelicalism and similar traditions. We were taught that our life's work was to convert as many people as possible to save them from hell. If our mission is not to save people for the afterlife, then what is it?

I like the interpretation of Marcus Borg, who says that the purpose of the church and the Christian religion is *transformation*—the transformation of individual lives and of the world.

In the Great Commission, Jesus said to make disciples and to *teach them what He commanded*. And what did Jesus command? Jesus summarized all the commands of scripture as loving God, and loving your neighbor as yourself.

You won't be able to authentically love your neighbor if your job is to save and change your neighbor. You won't be a good listener. You will miss out on the gifts they have to offer you, and the gift you're trying to offer them—a get-out-of-hell-free card—is no gift at all. But as we practice the way of Jesus, we will transform ourselves and transform our world. We will model what Martin Luther King Jr. called an "overriding loyalty to mankind" rather than loyalty to our sectional tribes.

When Thich Nhat Hanh visited the United States, he shared in the Eucharist with several of his new Christian friends. For many of us, the Lord's Supper was a moment of fear and condemnation. We were told to examine ourselves to see if we were really Christians or not. Many of us were afraid to partake at all, for fear that we would consume the body and blood of Christ "in an unworthy manner" (1 Corinthians 11:27). But as discussed in chapter 3, the great irony of using that passage as a warning is that Paul was condemning a divided church in which the rich enjoyed a private feast while the poor were left with scraps. It was the exclusivity of their meal that made it unworthy of Christ! Christ sets an open table for a global family to feast together as brothers and sisters.

Nhat Hanh reflected on Christian Communion, reminding us that this meal, which has so often been used to scare us and divide us, is actually held at a table set for all people, because it is the table of a universal God.

> *When Buddhists and Christians come together, we should share a meal in mindfulness as a deep practice of Communion. . . . This is Holy Communion, to live in faith. When we practice this way, every meal is the Last Supper. . . . When we eat together in this way, the food and the community of co-practitioners are the objects of our mindfulness. It is through the food and one another that the ultimate becomes present.*

When I was growing up, I felt alienated from my "unsaved" family members. In recent years, I have been able to reconnect with my aunts and uncles, and I have found that we have so much in common! I was unable to appreciate their love and wisdom when I was growing up because our family was too busy praying for them to get saved. Now that I've set aside my need to convert them, I can meet them at an open table. I can share my time with them in mindfulness and communion, as Nhat Hanh says. I can see the divine in them. We experience the beauty of mutuality, and our oneness reminds me that God is not owned by any people. We all need each other, and we are all in this together.

13.

A WAY OF LOVE

Connecting to God, Each Other, and Ourselves

You do not have to be good. . . .
You only have to let the soft animal of your body
love what it loves.

—**Mary Oliver**

As you might imagine, I get a good amount of criticism from evangelicals. But I'm also confronted by the occasional pushy atheist. I've been asked, "Why do you still call yourself a Christian at all? Why not just follow deconstruction to its obvious conclusion? It's the sunk-cost fallacy: You're only holding on to belief because you've put so much time in that it feels like a waste to throw it away. You think you need to retain part of it, but you don't. Be intellectually honest and just admit you don't believe!"

I get it. I've considered it. As a part of my deconstruction journey, in order to be intellectually honest, I had to allow nonbelief to be on the table as a legitimate option. And I fully respect people who chose that option. But personally, I can't get there. And no, it isn't just a sunk-cost fallacy. I still believe, because I believe we were made *for* love and *from* love—and although Christianity is far from the only way to live in connection to that love, the way of Jesus has helped me experience God's love in profound and unignorable ways.

In some ways, now that I've deconstructed conservative evangelicalism and set aside a need for certainty, a Bible without errors, and a faith with all the answers, my belief feels more vibrant and authentic than ever before. Before, I was disconnected from myself. I was taught my heart was wicked. I was not allowed to honor my intuition. Since I didn't know and love myself, I couldn't truly know and love God. I ended up finding God more deeply in the parts of myself that I wasn't previously allowed to listen to.

If you have begun to break away from high-control religion and a punishing God, I'm not here to tell you where you should land. If you don't want to return to church, even a more progressive one, I get it. It might feel like returning to the scene of the crime!

But there is one thing I know. You were made for love and connection. I believe you were made to connect with God, yourself, and others. More than that, I believe that we are already all connected to each other and to God, even though we are often totally unaware of it. Living disconnected, we are lonely. We are often, in the words of James Finley, "skimming over the surface of the depths of our own life, and hidden in the depths over which we are skimming is our oneness with God and with one another." For me now, spirituality is about entering those depths and experiencing and embodying those connections. Whatever makes me feel connected to myself, to God, and to others—this is spiritual for me.

Many of us have no idea what it looks like to live out this kind of spirituality because we have never known a spirituality without fear as its foundation. What does a relationship with God look like if God is not going to punish us? If we have never been given permission to truly love ourselves, it may feel wrong or selfish to start. And without the need to convert our neighbors, what is the purpose of church or the point of faith? I want to close this book by being very practical. I want to discuss how to bring the spirituality of love into our world, because I truly believe that we were made for this.

First, God.

GOD: A REINTRODUCTION

Some of us need to be wholly reintroduced to God. We have to start from scratch. God is not a big guy in the sky. We think we know this, but the subconscious assumption creeps back in. In truth, God is our *source*, a universal spirit of always-creating love to whom we are all connected. The very nature of reality is love. Richard Rohr says God is another name for reality: "reality with a personality." That means the very nature of reality is love. We are all connected together in God, and "God" is what we call the whole big connected thing. And that big connected thing is actually a *who*, because the big connected thing is Itself (Himself, Herself) *in relationship with us*. God is personal, and God is universal. My words fail. Paul did well when he recognized this universal truth in the words of a "pagan" Greek poet: In God, "we live and move and have our being" (Acts 17:28).

For many of us, fear of punishment was the fuel for our relationship with God. Coming into a relationship with God was about appeasing a tyrant. You had to get on his good side, because you didn't want to see what his bad side was like. You had to be born again in order to feel any sense of safety. But we don't need to *do anything* or *believe the right things* to be safe in the love of God. We are eternally safe in God.

For some of us, this is a brand-new paradigm.

Being "born again" is not a transactional affair. It doesn't change the way God sees you or your spiritual status, whether you're in or out. It doesn't change your eternal destiny. It is recognizing that you are already forgiven, you are already accepted, and you couldn't be any more accepted than you already are. You are already a part of God, and God has always been a part of you. Once, you were blind to this, but now you can see it.

One of the most powerful sermons I have ever read is from the great Paul Tillich. It's called "You Are Accepted." Tillich was a brilliant scholar and theologian with vast doctrinal knowledge, and yet, at the end of the day, his message about meeting God couldn't be simpler. Here is the powerful conclusion to his sermon:

> *Do we know what it means to be struck by grace? It does not mean that we suddenly believe that God exists, or that Jesus is the Saviour, or that the Bible contains the truth. . . .*
>
> *Grace strikes us when we are in great pain and restlessness . . . It strikes us when, year after year, the longed-for perfection of life does not appear, when the old compulsions reign within us as they have for decades, when despair destroys all joy and courage. Sometimes at that moment a wave of light breaks into our darkness, and it is as though a voice were saying: "You are accepted. You are accepted, accepted by that which is greater than you, and the name of which you do not know. . . . Do not try to do anything now; perhaps later you will do much. Do not seek for anything; do not perform anything; do not intend anything. Simply accept the fact that you are accepted!" If that happens to us, we experience grace. After such an experience we may not be better than before, and we may not believe more than before. But everything is transformed. In that moment, grace conquers sin, and reconciliation bridges the gulf of estrangement. And nothing is demanded of this experience, no religious or moral or intellectual presupposition, nothing but acceptance.*

If I am already accepted—God is not going to punish me—then what is my motivation for pursuing or loving God? Well, think about it like this: In our romantic lives, what motivates us to pursue love? Love itself does. *Love is its own reward.* When we are struck by grace and smitten by this unrelenting presence and unconditional love, something unlocks in us. It's the doorway to loving God.

I am reminded of Augustine of Hippo's moving love letter to God, mourning the time lost during the part of his life where he was unaware of his connection to God:

> *How late I came to love you, O Beauty so ancient and so fresh, how late I came to love you. You were within me, yet I had gone outside to seek you. . . . And always you were with me, I was not with you. All these beauties kept me far from you—although they would not have existed at all unless they had their being in you. You called, you cried, you shattered my deafness. You sparkled, you blazed, you drove away my blindness. . . . You touched me, and now I burn with longing.*

The moment of salvation Augustine describes has nothing to do with assenting to right doctrines about God. It is becoming aware of how God has always been within us.

But we are not always aware. God is present in all things, and everything has its being in God, but we are often blind to this reality. We are so distracted and numb, it's like we live much of our life in a trance, separated from love. But God does not punish us for being latecomers to love. The moment we turn toward God, we find that God is already running out to meet us, and when we have a genuine experience of the love of God, we "taste and see that the LORD is good" (Psalm

34:8). Working on our "personal relationship with God" does not do *anything* to change how accepted we are by God's limitless love. It only has to do with our awareness of that love.

LOVING GOD IS LOVING YOURSELF (AND EVERYTHING ELSE)

Being connected to God—which is the same thing as loving God—helps me to love myself and everyone else, because all of creation is in God and is beloved by God. Loving God reminds me that we are all a part of God, all connected together in God. This is why Jesus said that loving God was the first and greatest commandment.

When I had a punishing view of God, this commandment always bothered me. *Commanding* us to love God felt narcissistic. And if *some guy* commanded you to love him or else he'd torture you, it would be. But God *isn't* a big guy who throws tantrums when he isn't getting enough attention. We are commanded to love God because God is the connected nature of reality. Loving God is seeing God's Spirit in everyone and everything. We must "give glory" to God in everything, not because we'll hurt God's precious feelings if we don't, but because acknowledging the divine way that we're all connected is how we live in loving reality. Loving God is the greatest commandment because *loving God helps you love everyone and everything else*.

In fact, if your love of God *doesn't* cause you to more deeply love yourself and other people, then it's not actually God you're loving. It's probably some culturally constructed identity marker—an aspect of your ego. It is an idol.

The Jewish rabbi Abraham Heschel defined an idol as "any god who is mine but not yours, any god concerned with me but not with you." For Heschel, "to act in the spirit of religion is to unite what lies apart, to remember that humanity as a whole is God's beloved child."

When I am connected to the reality of my oneness with God, I am also aware of my neighbor's oneness with God. This helps me be ready to love my neighbor, because it helps me to see the divine in my neighbor—to see in my neighbor that which is "too beautiful to die."

Loving God also helps me fully embrace myself and all that God has created me to be. Thomas Merton tells us that this is the truth at the heart of spirituality: "If I find God, I will find myself. If I find myself, I will find God, that I join God in knowing who God knows me to be, hidden with Christ in God forever." Coming into remembrance of God's loving reality is what prayer and meditation are all about. Loving God helps us love all people and all creation.

It also works in the other direction. Loving people helps us love God. First John 4:20 says, "Whoever claims to love God yet hates a brother or sister is a liar." So we must love our neighbor in order to love God. And we must also love ourselves in order to love God and neighbor, for how can you love your neighbor *as yourself* if you do not even love yourself? All love hangs together! When we love our true divine self, we are loving God, just as when we recognize that deathless beauty in our neighbor, we love them—and we love God in them.

PERSONAL SPIRITUALITY: GROWING IN LOVE

Growing up in evangelicalism, I was encouraged to have a "daily quiet time." This essentially meant reading the Bible every day (aiming to read it through in a year if you wanted the most spiritual points) and praying. I often failed miserably at this. For many of us, a failure to have regular personal devotions was a source of guilt and shame. We thought we were not spiritual enough because we found the Bible boring and difficult to read or because we struggled to feel a sense of connectedness as we read.

This is nothing to feel guilty about. The Bible *can be* boring and difficult to read! Some parts are much more enlivening to the spirit than others. I still find life and beauty there, especially in the Psalms and the Gospels. I encounter wisdom in the parables of Jesus. The symbols, language, and metaphors of the Bible are not the only way to understand spirituality, but they are my mother tongue, and they still speak to me.

But reading the Bible is not the only way to personally connect with God. The Spirit of God is present in many spiritual writings. Read what leads you into the presence of love, whether it's the Bible or Rumi or Mary Oliver. Or don't read at all! For the first 1,500 years of the church, common people did not have access to the Bible and wouldn't have been able to read it even if they did—but they still had the Spirit of God. Opportunities to connect with God abundantly surround us. If reading or studying scripture leads your spirit into connection with the great mystery of love at the heart of all things, then by all means, keep that spiritual practice. But if not, then find the practices that make you bloom.

My friend Kevin Garcia, a queer, nonbinary spiritual mystic, wrote a beautiful book called *What Makes You Bloom*, in which they expound on practices such as rest, imagination, friendship, solidarity, generosity, radical honesty, defenselessness, kindness, unbearable compassion, patience, forgiveness, acceptance, grief, joy, pleasure, and wonder. Kevin describes a spiritual practice as "the thing you do each day, allowing you to enter into your awareness of Love's presence. This is the pathway toward finding our way back to Love, God, and Heaven because it shows us we never left. We just forgot."

The purpose of our spiritual life and practices is not to ensure that we go about every day believing the correct doctrines. We do not pray so that we have the correct theology in mind as we attend to our daily tasks. I meditate, pray, and seek union with God so that I can go out into the world mindfully connected to the love that fills me and all things, the love that binds us all together into one big connected thing. I am more joyful, more purposeful, more present when I am remembering the reality of my connection to God: that God is not far from any one of us. God is right here.

When you are truly experiencing communion with God through your spiritual practices, you will also be communing with your truest self—the image of God in you. You will know this is happening because you will love yourself without shame and without the sense that you should be careful not to love yourself too much. There will be nothing narcissistic about it, because you will realize that your love for yourself is also love for God and everyone else, and that God wants you to shine brightly as your truest self. This is the way that you, uniquely you, give glory to God. As Mary Oliver wrote in her holy poem, "Wild Geese," "You do not have to be good. . . . You only have to let the soft animal of your body love what it loves."

We can trust ourselves, and we must learn to listen to the holy part of ourselves, or we will never learn to listen to God. But we must never go it alone.

We are not isolated spiritual beings; we are knit together, and we need each other. Belonging to a church or a spiritual community is a spiritual practice because it reminds us of this truth that we are prone to forget.

But I have found this connection in other places as well. I recently began attending an ecstatic dance group in Raleigh.

Ecstatic dance is a free-form conscious dance, where there are no rules for movement. You feel the music, and feel your body and emotions, and feel your connection to the group, and you do what feels right for you.

When I went to my first gathering, in a large field at a local park, I was struggling to feel present in my body, and I thought this could potentially be a helpful practice for me. After nervously kicking off my shoes into the grass, I entered the group, sitting in a circle, where we received some brief instruction. Gino, the organizer, told us to let go of judgments and expectations, and honor whatever the moment brought to us. He encouraged us to trust ourselves and trust the journey we would be on. He told us to be conscious of each other, and if we wanted to dance with someone, to be mindful of the spirit of consent. This felt very different from the evangelical church announcements I was used to.

The music began softly, and I moved carefully, feeling my feet in the grass. As the electronic beats began to drop, I tried to give myself to the music without thinking too much about how silly I was sure I looked. Over the next ninety minutes, I went back and forth between feeling self-conscious and totally losing myself in the music and the communal rush. I felt a deep sense that even though we were all dancing in our own way, we were all part of one big connected thing.

Everyone danced their own dance, and yet we all danced together. I realized that in order to be true to this community, I must first be true to myself. The way we honor our community is not by diminishing ourselves but by shining our brightest and bringing our very best to others. Those who love us rejoice over us when we show up as our truest and best selves.

At the height of the set, during a crescendo of sound and movement, Anna, a florist in the group, began tossing flower petals in the air from a basket she had brought. They swirled around us as we reached our hands upward and our bodies surged together. One of the only rules is you aren't supposed to talk during the dance, but I heard someone say, "This is heaven!" I looked up and around, seeing everyone's hands lifted to swirling petals, and I immediately agreed.

After the music, we sat back down and went around the circle, sharing about our time together, Quaker style. Whatever was in your heart and spirit to share. Some people shared about the day they'd been having and the emotions they worked through as they wordlessly danced. Without hearing a sentence of preaching, some people shared that they forgave people they needed to forgive as they danced. Some people shared that they felt able to love themselves. One dear nonbinary dancer who looked to be in their mid-twenties stopped me in my tracks when they said, "Fifteen-year-old me would be so proud of me. I didn't know that I'd be alive at this age, much less this happy. Thank you all so much for making such a safe and supportive space for me to be my fullest self."

Make no mistake, that dance group was a spiritual community, every bit as much as a church—more so than many churches. At one point, while we were dancing and experiencing the palpable sense of oneness, I was struck by the thought that if any of us in this group discovered that one of us had a great need, surely we would come together to meet it. Our solidarity seemed obvious while I was in that state of connected bliss. Afterward, Anna told me, "My favorite part of the dance is when I remember that we are all dancing together, and by 'we,' I mean everyone on planet Earth."

This ecstatic dance group did not have any doctrine, but they had love. They did not have a statement of faith, but there was mutuality, care, and connection. People felt supported. They were given permission to be their own guides. People were being healed in this community, not because it gave them the correct answers or forced them to conform to a standard of belief or practice but because it was a place where they were unconditionally accepted. It invited them to make space for every part of their wild, beautiful selves. After our time together, we felt close to ourselves and closer to each other, and the way I see it, closer to God.

I don't care if you go to a Christian church or not, but everyone needs a supportive community, and everyone needs connection. Many of us are afraid of religious or spiritual communities because of our past church experiences. We've been in bad churches that kept people out who didn't conform. Many of us are afraid of spiritual communities because we assume they're all like that. But the way I see it, if a place believes that only they have the answers and everyone else is damned, that's not a true spiritual community; that is a fundamentalist cult. Superiority, exclusion, and division are exactly the opposite of true spirituality.

A spiritual community should be a place of discovery and curiosity. It can be a place where we connect with one another and with our spiritual ancestors by exploring ancient texts like the Bible, but it can also be a place where we learn how to listen to ourselves for the Spirit of God. A healthy spiritual leader helps you be attuned to what God is already saying to you through your own life and experiences. The church has not always been this kind of healthy community. Dogmatic and harsh, it has crushed people under its unbending "truth," and often it has forgotten how to love. But there is still hope for the church.

AN INCLUSIVE AND LIBERATIVE CHURCH

I have not given up on the church. Many churches and denominations are moving in the direction of love and inclusivity. I currently attend an inclusive United Methodist Church. In May 2024, we celebrated together that the Methodist denomination officially repealed all bans on the celebration and affirmation of same-sex unions. I think this is beautiful, but I can also see why a queer person may not feel safe in a space that only came to this position of inclusivity so recently after such an uphill battle.

If the church is to have a future of love and connection, it must be a repentant church. It must be a church that centers the people it has excluded. If Christian leaders welcome queer people into the church only to pat themselves on the back for being inclusive, they're missing the point. As my friend Stan Mitchell says, queer-affirming churches are not exactly doing a good thing—they just stopped doing a bad thing. If you're beating someone, you don't get to congratulate yourself as compassionate for stopping your assault. Unfortunately, Christian churches have been sources of harm and exclusion for many, especially for queer people. Following the way of Jesus would mean to put those who were last, first.*

One of the themes of this book is that centering the afterlife in our spirituality takes our eyes off of this life, which is not what Jesus did. Jesus lived and died for the kingdom of God. Christians, including evangelicals, often excel at individual acts of charity. But the kingdom of God is not about charity. It's about changing the structures of the world so that it works for the least of these.

Martin Luther King Jr.'s vision of "the beloved community," which is similar to Jesus's vision of "the kingdom of God," was rooted in fighting what he saw as the three great

---

* Many churches are seeking to be places of connection, not punishment. Resources like gaychurch.org and churchclarity.org help to find churches that are safe spaces for queer people—which is often a good indicator that the church is on a path of inclusion in other areas as well.

evils facing our society: racism, militarism, and income inequality. All three are alive and well in the American Empire. I would also add sexism and queerphobia to King's list. These are powers of darkness and forces that disconnect us, and the way of Jesus is to oppose these forces with an alternate kingdom that puts our belovedness and connectedness on display.

But these oppressive forces are constantly pushing back and seeking to shape our desires and disconnect us. This is why we cannot do it alone. We would be swallowed back up in it. Bell hooks puts it this way: "To build community requires vigilant awareness of the work we must continually do to undermine all the socialization that leads us to behave in ways that perpetuate domination." In a world of domination, our communities must constantly remind us that we are all part of this together.

This can mean many things. My pastor friend Melissa and her church, Raleigh Mennonite Church, are on the front lines of every protest, fighting for a better world. When our North Carolina Lieutenant Governor Mark Robinson called trans and queer people "filth" in a public speech, Melissa helped organize a protest outside of his office. Queer adults and children from her church held up signs proudly declaring their belovedness: *I am not filth. I am God's child.*

In a time when democratic norms are being eroded and national politics seem hopelessly gridlocked, churches can be powerful local hubs for community organizing, bringing people together across lines of race and class to build collective power. Pastors and spiritual leaders should be loud voices on issues of justice and structural inequality. They can and should fight for the end of the death penalty, which is rooted in retributive justice, which is no justice at all, and disproportionately kills minorities and the poor. They can and should fight for universal health care, for a living wage, and for racial justice.

I previously mentioned that in Luke 4, Jesus linked his ministry to the ancient biblical law stipulating that every fiftieth year would be a Jubilee, when wealth and land were to be redistributed, debts were to be forgiven, and enslaved people were to be set free. Jesus did not have political power, so he did not institute a legal Jubilee. Instead, he gathered people into a new community that was defined by the *values* of the Jubilee: liberation and equality. A community shaped by those values would not have to free slaves every fifty years, because it would liberate people and never enslave them again. Debts would not have to be repeatedly erased in a community where people no longer make debtors out of others. The poor would not need a massive redistribution of wealth every fifty years in a community of radical sharing. The church should be a mutual aid society, where these values of solidarity are being put into practice.

It is no surprise that after Jesus died and his followers formed the first Christian community, the very first thing they did was radically share all their property and possessions:

> *All who believed were together and had all things in common; they would sell their possessions and goods and distribute the proceeds to all, as any had need. . . . Now the whole group of those who believed were of one heart and soul, and no one claimed private ownership of any possessions, but everything they owned was held in common.*
>
> Acts 2:44–45, 4:32, NRSV

Jesus's early followers understood the assignment. Jesus was passionate about liberation in this life—for all of society, not just for individuals for the afterlife. Jesus wanted a new world that worked for everyone.

The church can still live out this ethos. My friend John started a church that made debt cancellation a regular practice in their Sunday service. When they pay off a debt, the pastor states, "As members of Christ's body, we are called to cancel debts" and asks the recipient, "Will you give us the gift of letting us cancel yours?" The member responds, "I will, thanks be to God."

One of the first candidates for this practice, drowning in credit card debt, recalled feeling hesitant. "Aren't there other people who deserve it more than me?" he asked. In evangelical (and American) culture, credit card debt is often viewed as a personal failing rather than a symptom of capitalism. My friend reminded him that as a church family, they were all in this together, and that meant they tried their best to carry each other's burdens. It is our privilege to do so because it reminds us that we do not deserve to be punished. We deserve grace, and it is our joy to offer grace to one another. Practices like this remind us that when one person is hurting, we all hurt, because we are all connected.

Those of us who say we follow Jesus should still be seeking the kingdom of God—the beloved community—and we can begin by building communities of liberation, care, and mutuality. In a community like this, everyone belongs. We can passionately worship the God revealed in Jesus Christ without having to demand doctrinal conformity. The purpose is our love and connection with one another, not our statement of faith.

Some spiritual communities tend to excel in personal piety, spiritual disciplines, and ecstatic devotion. Others are more action-oriented, focused on acts of justice and service. I believe that when we are truly living in love and connection, both will come naturally. Our loving connection to God thrusts us out into the world to love.

As we consider what the purpose of Christian spirituality is, if it's not to avoid punishment, I submit it is this: to be transformed, individually and communally, into people of love. Our communities will be marked by mutuality and solidarity, not uniformity. We hold one another as family.

If your faith and spirituality were bent by hell, twisted by fear and punishment, I am truly sorry, and I feel your pain firsthand. But I also know God is a master at wringing good out of bad. The story of your spirituality is unfinished. The first act may have started out with fear, but it doesn't have to end that way. You may wish you could go back and change your path, but then you would lose who you are now. Your path has brought you here. As the delusion of separateness lifts, you may even come to appreciate the winding path that brought you here. The delightful freedom of your unconditional acceptance can be all the sweeter because of how stale the prison of your fear once was.

Now is a time for excitement. Without the shroud of punishment, we are invited to explore the beautiful world that opens up before us. You are not bound to your past. Your spirituality does not have to conform to the patterns you were raised with. You are able to listen to your wild, wise heart. You are able to hear the voice of God. God is not disappointed in you and is not going to punish you for straying outside of the lines. You are invited to follow the Spirit with courage, curiosity, and compassion into a love without fear.

May it be so.

Like a good (ex-)pastor, allow me to close in prayer.

I pray that . . . you may be strengthened in your inner being with power through [God's] Spirit, and that Christ may dwell in your hearts through faith, as you are being rooted and grounded in love. I pray that you may have the power to comprehend, with all the saints, what is the breadth and length and height and depth, and to know the love of Christ that surpasses knowledge, so that you may be filled with all the fullness of God.

Ephesians 3:16–19, NRSV

Amen.

ACKNOWLEDGMENTS

Thank you to my parents, who love me enough that I know I can disappoint them without having to question their acceptance of me. Thank you to my brother Daniel and sister Rachel, who found their own ways out of a spirituality of hell—I hope our friendship continues to deepen on this side of deconstruction.

Thank you to Tom Tapping, who taught me to sing my own song.

Thank you to Emily, who was my ride or die through an important stretch of my life, and who partnered with me in our escape from evangelicalism. I'm glad to have you as a friend. And thank you to my rescue pitty, Maev, my ride or die through this next stretch of my life, and my companion on the walks where many of the ideas of this book took shape.

To Judah, Remy, Royal, and Carmen, thank you for giving me a visceral and urgent reason to care about becoming a more loving person, and to contribute to a more loving world.

Thank you to my editor, Lauren O'Neal, who brought not only her editorial eye to this manuscript but also her heart for the people left out of evangelicalism. Thank you to my agent, David Morris, a wise advisor and friend.

Thank you to so many friends. Dustin Smith, Burton Buffaloe, you stood with me when I was going through hell and your compassion saved me. Thank you to Tim Kennard, Meg Holiday, Archer Knightly, and all my other dear queer friends who show me what it looks like to be your true, unashamed self. Thank you to Keri Ladouceur, for chatting through many of these topics over the course of dozens of conversations with countless open tabs to still explore. Thanks to the Hulkamania bro groupchat, for the memes, lols, and encouragement.

Thank you to Scarlett Longstreet, my unequally yoked one in eight billion, who shares my belief that this whole thing is about love and connection or it doesn't matter at all.

NOTES

CHAPTER 1

7   **However, he made it clear:** Timothy Keller, "The Importance of Hell," *Timothy Keller* (blog), August 1, 2008, https://timothykeller.com/blog/2008/8/1/the-importance -of-hell.

10   **"I don't respect that":** Penn Jillette, "Not Proselytize," posted November 13, 2009, by Rich Maurer, YouTube, 53 sec., https://www.youtube.com/watch?v=owZc3X q8obk.

CHAPTER 2

21   **Psychiatrist M. Scott Peck beautifully:** M. Scott Peck, *The Road Less Traveled: A New Psychology of Love, Traditional Values and Spiritual Growth* (New York: Simon and Schuster, 1978), 81.

24   **As Franciscan priest and author:** Richard Rohr, *The Universal Christ: How a Forgotten Reality Can Change Everything We See, Hope For, and Believe* (New York: Convergent Books, 2019), 181.

25   **As feminist theorist bell hooks:** bell hooks, *All About Love: New Visions* (New York: William Morrow, 2000), 17–18.

25   **Hooks writes of an encounter:** hooks, *All About Love*, 21.

CHAPTER 3

41   **In her book *Good Inside*:** Becky Kennedy, *Good Inside: A Guide to Becoming the Parent You Want to Be* (New York: Harper Wave, 2022), 7.

41   **Megan Von Fricken, a therapist:** Megan Von Fricken, Instagram photo, March 12, 2024, https://www.instagram .com/p/C4acChOudkM/.

42   **Kennedy points out that:** Kennedy, *Good Inside*, 6.

42   **"In our early years":** Kennedy, *Good Inside*, 7.

42   **Kennedy writes that in order:** Kennedy, *Good Inside*, 8.

43   **As Richard Rohr says:** Richard Rohr, *The Universal Christ: How a Forgotten Reality Can Change Everything We See, Hope For, and Believe* (New York: Convergent Books, 2019), 62.

CHAPTER 4

57   **As Richard Rohr has said:** Richard Rohr, *The Universal Christ: How a Forgotten Reality Can Change Everything We See, Hope For, and Believe* (New York: Convergent Books, 2019), 177.

CHAPTER 5

68   **The Bible scholar Pete Enns:** Pete Enns, *The Bible Tells Me So: Why Defending Scripture Has Made Us Unable to Read It* (San Francisco: HarperOne, 2014), 20.

69   **Following his conscience:** Enns, *The Bible Tells Me So*, 20.

69   **His pastoral team quit:** Ira Glass, host, *This American Life*, podcast, episode 304, "Heretics," aired December 16, 2005, https://www.thisamericanlife.org/304/transcript.

69   Even his mentee: Glass, *This American Life*.

74   I love how the late: Rachel Held Evans, *A Year of Biblical Womanhood: How a Liberated Woman Found Herself Sitting on Her Roof, Covering Her Head, and Calling Her Husband "Master"* (Nashville: Thomas Nelson, 2012), 296.

CHAPTER 6

82   In fact, theologian David Bentley Hart: David Bentley Hart, *That All Shall Be Saved: Heaven, Hell, and Universal Salvation* (New Haven: Yale University Press, 2019), 107.

89   Many preachers have tried: Klyne R. Snodgrass, *Stories with Intent: A Comprehensive Guide to the Parables of Jesus*, 2nd ed. (Grand Rapids, MI: William B. Eerdmans Publishing Company, 2018), 426.

91   As biblical scholar Nik Ansell: Nik Ansell, "Hell: The Nemesis of Hope?," *The Other Journal*, April 20, 2009, https://theotherjournal.com/2009/04/hell-the-nemesis-of-hope/. For an account of every time Jesus uses the word *Gehenna*, see Andrew Perriman, *Hell and Heaven in Narrative Perspective*, 2nd ed. (pub. by author, 2021).

92   In fact, the contemporary: Josephus, "The Jewish War," in Josephus: *The Jewish War*, vol. 3, Books 5–7, trans. H. St. J. Thackeray, Loeb Classical Library 210 (Cambridge, MA: Harvard University Press, 1928), 5.518.

93   Theologian Harold Wells explains: Harold Wells, *A Future for Socialism? Christian Socialism for a Post-Communist Era* (Cleveland: Pilgrim Press, 1996), 39.

95   Richard Rohr says that "we": Richard Rohr, *Falling Upward: A Spirituality for the Two Halves of Life* (San Francisco: Jossey-Bass, 2011), 57.

96   "And now," he concludes: Rev. Jeremiah A. Wright Jr., "America's Chickens Coming Home to Roost," posted October 4, 2014, by The Orchard Enterprises, YouTube, 58:52, https://www.youtube.com/watch?v=UUtZNQ0REFA.

CHAPTER 7

102 **If evangelicals are going:** This line of reasoning draws on David Bentley Hart, *That All Shall Be Saved: Heaven, Hell, and Universal Salvation* (New Haven: Yale University Press, 2019), 101–2.

112 **The Hebrew Bible scholar:** Walter Brueggemann, quoted in Bradley Jersak, *Her Gates Will Never Be Shut: Hope, Hell, and the New Jerusalem* (Eugene, OR: Wipf and Stock, 2009), 93.

112 **Richard Rohr points out that "God":** Richard Rohr, *The Universal Christ: How a Forgotten Reality Can Change Everything We See, Hope For, and Believe* (New York: Convergent Books, 2019), 183.

115 **He said, "Forgiveness":** Desmond Tutu, *The Book of Forgiving: The Fourfold Path for Healing Ourselves and Our World* (San Francisco: HarperOne, 2014), 93.

116 **As the poet and environmental activist:** Wendell Berry, *Citizenship Papers: Essays* (Brooklyn, NY: Counterpoint Press, 2004), 25.

116 **As I've said, I don't:** I was first made aware of this interpretation of the passage by Jersak, *Her Gates Will Never Be Shut*, chap. 12.

CHAPTER 8

126 **The things we *think*:** Shunryū Suzuki, *Zen Mind, Beginner's Mind*, ed. Trudy Dixon (New York: Weatherhill, 1970), 21.

127 **The wonderful theologian:** Eugene F. Rogers Jr., *Elements of Christian Thought: A Basic Course in Christianese* (Minneapolis: Fortress Press, 2021), 1.

127 **In her poem:** Mary Oliver, "The World I Live In," in *Devotions: The Selected Poems of Mary Oliver* (New York: Penguin Press, 2017), 5.

129 In his book *The Four Agreements*: Don Miguel Ruiz, *The Four Agreements: A Practical Guide to Personal Freedom* (San Rafael, CA: Amber-Allen Publishing, 1997), 5.

129 Ruiz puts it this way: Don Miguel Ruiz, *The Mastery of Love: A Practical Guide to the Art of Relationship* (San Rafael, CA: Amber-Allen Publishing, 1999), 9.

130 Here are Katie's four questions: Byron Katie, *Loving What Is: Four Questions That Can Change Your Life* (New York: Harmony Books, 2002), 15.

132 After you investigate: Katie, *Loving What Is*, 5.

134 Richard Rohr points out that John: Richard Rohr, *The Universal Christ: How a Forgotten Reality Can Change Everything We See, Hope For, and Believe* (New York: Convergent Books, 2019), 60.

134 But as Rohr says, "How": Rohr, *The Universal Christ*, 66.

CHAPTER 9

143 In his book *The Spirituals*: James H. Cone, *The Spirituals and the Blues: An Interpretation* (Maryknoll, NY: Orbis Books, 1991), 88–90.

144 Douglas writes that: Kelly Brown Douglas, *The Black Christ* (Maryknoll, NY: Orbis Books, 1994), 7.

145 For them, the cross was: Douglas, *The Black Christ*, 17.

147 The theologian Jürgen Moltmann writes: Jürgen Moltmann, *The Way of Jesus Christ: Christology in Messianic Dimensions*, trans. Margaret Kohl (Minneapolis: Fortress Press, 1993), 274.

149 The popular evangelical scholar: N.T. Wright, *The Day the Revolution Began: Reconsidering the Meaning of Jesus's Crucifixion* (New York: HarperOne, 2016), 75.

150 In Jesus's day: Marcus J. Borg, *The Heart of Christianity: Rediscovering a Life of Faith* (New York: HarperOne, 2003), 132.

151 **Food scarcity and indebtedness:** Borg, *The Heart of Christianity*, 133–34.

151 **Even in the richest:** "Facts About Child Hunger," Feeding America, accessed May 14, 2024, https://www.feedingamerica .org/hunger-in-america/child-hunger-facts.

151 **During the COVID-19 pandemic:** Chuck Collins, Omar Ocampo, and Sophia Paslaski, "Billionaire Bonanza 2020: Wealth Windfalls, Tumbling Taxes, and Pandemic Profiteers," Institute for Policy Studies, April 23, 2020, https://ips-dc.org/wp-content/uploads/2020/04/Billionaire -Bonanza-2020.pdf.

154 **The mujerista theologian:** Ada María Isasi-Díaz, *En la Lucha / In the Struggle: Elaborating a Mujerista Theology*, 10th anniversary edition (Minneapolis: Fortress Press, 2004).

155 **It's "inclusion with":** Heard in a talk by SueAnn Shiah at the Post-Evangelical Collective gathering, April 2024.

156 **Martin Luther King Jr. preached:** Martin Luther King Jr., "On Being a Good Neighbor," in *Strength to Love* (Minneapolis: Fortress Press, 2010), 24.

156 **King concludes his sermon:** King, *Strength to Love*, 30.

157 **King fought for this dream:** Martin Luther King Jr., *Stride Toward Freedom: The Montgomery Story* (New York: Harper & Brothers, 1958), 215.

157 **Kurt Marti, a Swiss pastor:** Kurt Marti, *Gott im Ungefähren* (Zurich: Kataloge der Edition, 1971), 35. Quote translated by Andrea Moussanet.

CHAPTER 10

162 **Unless we come to grips:** Timothy Keller, "The Importance of Hell," *Timothy Keller* (blog), August 1, 2008, https://timothykeller.com/blog/2008/8/1/the-importance -of-hell.

166 Theologian Marcus Borg points out: Marcus J. Borg, *The Heart of Christianity: Rediscovering a Life of Faith* (New York: HarperOne, 2003), 95.

169 He called that moment: James H. Cone, *The Cross and the Lynching Tree* (Maryknoll, NY: Orbis Books, 2011), 78.

169 King said, "I experienced": Cone, *The Cross and the Lynching Tree*, 78.

169 But from his bombed-out: Cone, *The Cross and the Lynching Tree*, 79.

171 In a letter to his wife: Cone, *The Cross and the Lynching Tree*, 81.

172 Richard Rohr teaches: Richard Rohr, *A Spring Within Us: A Book of Daily Meditations* (Albuquerque, NM: CAC Publishing, 2016), 122.

173 I like how Marcus Borg: Borg, *The Heart of Christianity*, 88.

174 Even our worst enemies: Martin Luther King Jr., *Strength to Love* (Minneapolis: Fortress Press, 2010), 46.

174 He preached, "Love": King, *Strength to Love*, 48.

174 He knew that the only: King, *Strength to Love*, 50.

177 In his powerful book: Jürgen Moltmann, *The Crucified God: The Cross of Christ as the Foundation and Criticism of Christian Theology*, trans. R. A. Wilson and John Bowden (Minneapolis: Fortress Press, 1993), 246.

177 Theologian James Cone draws: Cone, *The Cross and the Lynching Tree*, 31.

177 The haunting piece: Lorenzo Harris, "Christmas in Georgia, A.D. 1916," *The Crisis* 13, no. 2 (1916): 78–79, https://modjourn.org/issue/bdr510308/.

178 But as Cone writes: Cone, *The Cross and the Lynching Tree*, 23.

179 **Father Gregory Boyle says:** Gregory Boyle, *Tattoos on the Heart: The Power of Boundless Compassion* (New York: Free Press, 2010), 172.

179 **One piece of evidence:** Matthias Roberts, *Holy Runaways: Rejecting the Harm, Reclaiming the Holy* (Austin, TX: Worthy Books, 2023), 192.

180 **In the United States, trans:** Jennifer L. Truman and Rachel E. Morgan, "Violent Victimization by Sexual Orientation and Gender Identity, 2017–2020," Bureau of Justice Statistics, June 2022, https://bjs.ojp.gov/library /publications/violent-victimization-sexual-orientation-and -gender-identity-2017-2020.

180 **Worse, the number:** C. Mandler, "Murders of Trans People Nearly Doubled Over Past 4 Years, and Black Trans Women Are Most at Risk, Report Finds," CBS News, October 13, 2022, https://www.cbsnews.com/news/transgender -community-murder-rates-everytown-for-gun-safety-report/.

180 **In 2024, there were 669:** "Anti-Transgender Legislation in 2024," Trans Legislation Tracker, accessed October 26, 2024, https://translegislation.com/.

CHAPTER 11

187 **Joseph Campbell famously said:** Joseph Campbell and Bill Moyers, *The Power of Myth*, ed. Betty Sue Flowers (New York: Anchor Books, 1991), 206.

190 **Remember what clinical:** Becky Kennedy, *Good Inside: A Guide to Becoming the Parent You Want to Be* (New York: Harper Wave, 2022), 7.

193 **By the second half:** Richard Rohr, *The Divine Dance: The Trinity and Your Transformation* (New Kensington, PA: Whitaker House, 2016), 63.

194 **Borg writes, "We are":** Marcus J. Borg, *The God We Never Knew: Beyond Dogmatic Religion to a More Authentic Contemporary Faith* (New York: HarperOne, 1997), 31.

CHAPTER 12

197 **Nhat Hanh later wrote:** Thich Nhat Hanh, *Living Buddha, Living Christ* (New York: Riverhead Books, 1995), 5–6.

197 **In a staggering statement:** Thomas Merton, *Faith and Violence: Christian Teaching and Christian Practice* (Notre Dame, IN: University of Notre Dame Press, 1968), 106.

204 **Biblical scholar Marcus Borg:** Marcus Borg, *Jesus: A New Vision* (San Francisco: Harper & Row, 1987), 175.

207 **When Jesus said "I am:** Nhat Hanh, *Living Buddha, Living Christ*, 56.

209 **As D. Danyelle Thomas powerfully:** D. Danyelle Thomas, *The Day God Saw Me as Black: The Journey to Liberated Faith* (New York: Row House Publishing, 2024), 36.

210 **We will model:** "Martin Luther King, Jr.'s Nobel Peace Prize Lecture from Oslo, 11 Dec. 1964 (full audio)," posted January 20, 2016, by Nobel Prize, YouTube, 52:42, https://www.youtube.com/watch?v=u71K76y7jf8.

211 **When Buddhists and Christians:** Nhat Hanh, *Living Buddha, Living Christ*, 32.

CHAPTER 13

216 **We are often, in the words:** James Finley, host *Turning to the Mystics*, podcast, "Thomas Merton: Session 4," Center for Action and Contemplation, May 9, 2020, https://cac.org/podcasts/thomas-merton-session-4/.

217 **Richard Rohr says God:** "Richard Rohr," interview by Scott Brown, *Conversations with Masters*, Stagen, accessed August 28, 2024, https://stagen.com/wisdom/richard-rohr/.

218 **Do we know:** Paul Tillich, *The Shaking of the Foundations* (New York: Charles Scribner's Sons, 1948), 162–63.

219 **How late I:** Augustine of Hippo, *The Confessions*, trans. Maria Boulding (New York: New City Press, 1997), Book X, Chapter 27, Paragraph 38.

220 **The Jewish rabbi:** Abraham Joshua Heschel, *The Insecurity of Freedom: Essays on Human Existence* (New York: Farrar, Straus & Giroux, 1966), 72.

220 **For Heschel, "to act":** Heschel, *The Insecurity of Freedom*, 82.

221 **This helps me:** Gabriel Marcel, paraphrased quote. Source is uncertain.

221 **Thomas Merton tells us:** James Finley, paraphrasing Thomas Merton, "Thomas Merton: Session 4," *Turning to the Mystics* (podcast), Center for Action and Contemplation, May 9, 2020, accessed May 14, 2024, https://cac.org/podcast/thomas-merton-session-4/.

222 **Kevin describes a spiritual practice:** Kevin Garcia, *What Makes You Bloom: Cultivating a Practice for Connecting with Your Divine Self* (Minneapolis: Broadleaf Books, 2024), 16.

228 **Bell hooks puts it:** bell hooks, *Teaching Community: A Pedagogy of Hope* (New York: Routledge, 2003), 36.

INDEX

ABOUT THE AUTHOR

Brian Recker, MDiv, is a public theologian, speaker, and writer on Christian spirituality without exclusionary dogma. The son of a Baptist preacher and an alum of the fundamentalist Bob Jones University, he spent eight years as an evangelical pastor before deconstructing his faith to find a more inclusive spirituality. He now speaks and writes about rethinking Christian spirituality on his popular Instagram account and his Substack, *Beloved*. He lives in Raleigh, North Carolina, and has four children and a rescue pup named Maev.

01 14